DAILY DEW

Let my teaching fall like rain and my words descend like dew,
like showers on new grass, like abundant rain on tender plants.
Deuteronomy 32:2

GREGORY T. HOLLIS

Heartfelt Dedication & Thanks...

To my Lord & Savior Jesus Christ who radically revolutionized my life from early on and gave me a powerful reason to live!

To my parents...Jonathan & Arlene Hollis who gave me a rock solid foundation to build on...my life and ministry is eternally etched with your imprint. I'm forever grateful for the godly example you've been...actions really do speak louder than words!

To my in-laws...Dave & Judy Kyllonen for raising one amazing woman of God and for your godly influence in my life and ministry. You have blessed me more than you know!

To Kristie...the love of my life, my faithful ministry partner, the most amazing mother of our children and passionate lover of your crazy dogs. You ignite me! You give me a reason to get out of bed everyday. Your passion for God and for life is contagious. I'm blessed to have found you over 30 years ago. What a journey we've been on. Thank you for joining me on this wonderful adventure we call life...the best is yet to come!

To my children...Elijah Tyrone & Ashlee, Isaiah Threll & Brittany and Alexsondra Kabri...You make me smile every day and give me pride that only a blessed father can know. I'm privileged to work alongside you in reaching this world for Jesus Christ!

To my grandchildren who are almost here...Zion Dainger and London Tara...this book is for you to someday hold in your hand and glean a little bit of wisdom from. I pray that your parents will raise you better than we raised them! I love you already and I haven't even met you yet. Coogi & Mooki are anxiously awaiting your arrival!

To Tim Enloe... You are more than a brother-in-law...you are a true friend. Thank you for your expertise and guidance. You are a blessing on so many levels to me. Thanks for always being there!

To all those who have poured your wisdom into my life...you know who you are. Great days are ahead as we follow His lead!

"Why we've lost our children!"

2 Chronicles 29:1-11

1 Hezekiah was twenty-five years old when he became king, and he reigned in Jerusalem twenty-nine years. His mother's name was Abijah daughter of Zechariah. 2 He did what was right in the eyes of the LORD, just as his father David had done. 3 In the first month of the first year of his reign, he opened the doors of the temple of the LORD and repaired them. 4 He brought in the priests and the Levites, assembled them in the square on the east side 5 and said: "Listen to me, Levites! Consecrate yourselves now and consecrate the temple of the LORD, the God of your fathers. Remove all defilement from the sanctuary. 6 Our fathers were unfaithful; they did evil in the eyes of the LORD our God and forsook him. They turned their faces away from the LORD's dwelling place and turned their backs on him. 7 They also shut the doors of the portico and put out the lamps. They did not burn incense or present any burnt offerings at the sanctuary to the God of Israel. 8 Therefore, the anger of the LORD has fallen on Judah and Jerusalem; he has made them an object of dread and horror and scorn, as you can see with your own eyes. 9 This is why our fathers have fallen by the sword and why our sons and daughters and our wives are in captivity. 10 Now I intend to make a covenant with the LORD, the God of Israel, so that his fierce anger will turn away from us. 11 My sons, do not be negligent now, for the LORD has chosen you to stand before him and serve him, to minister before him and to burn incense."

I guess the thing that bothers me the most sometimes, is the fact that so many of the children and young people that have grown up in church and in supposedly "Christian families", are walking away from the Lord in droves and are bound in captivity to sin. When I was a youth pastor, it always amazed me to find teenagers who lived in "godly" homes, but were rebellious towards the things of God. When I was able to venture a peek inside the life of their homes it became all too clear that what was "shown" on Sunday was not what was "lived" on the home front.

Hezekiah did what was right in the eyes of the Lord, and as he did he realized that the House of the Lord was in shambles. The leaders/fathers had turned their backs on the Lord and become unfaithful. Everything that should have been taken care of was neglected. The outcome was awful, yet predictable. Any time we neglect to follow the Lord and His ways, we position ourselves for disaster and trouble! And it's not just us who receive the punishment…it's our families. We stumble and fall and do stupid stuff and our families go into captivity because of our lame choices to do our own thing apart from the wisdom of God.

I don't know about you, but I want my family to be able to live a free, unencumbered life and to follow the Lord with all their hearts! I want them to live in the Lord's Favor and Blessing! I want to provide the atmosphere that will bring them blessings beyond measure! You and I have the privilege and responsibility to bless them in this way. Why not decide today to make a covenant before the Lord to get back on track and to make the right thing the main thing? Remove the things that need to be removed. Establish the things that need to be established…prayer, reading the Word, giving, etc. May we, like Hezekiah, decide to do what is right in the Lord's eyes and do whatever it takes to see that our families don't find themselves in captivity any longer! It's time to repair the things that are broken down and in shambles. God wants your family to succeed and He has the wisdom to help you know what to do and how to do it!

Why don't you pray a simple prayer with me today and follow it with obedience to the Lord? You and your family will be glad you did!

"Dear Lord Jesus, help me to always do what is right in Your eyes. Keep my heart pure as I follow Your lead. Forgive me where I've gotten off track, please help me to see clearly and to allow Your Holy Spirit to gently nudge me back on track so that I and those who follow me can be blessed by Your mighty hand! And if a gentle nudge doesn't work, go ahead and smack me harder until I listen and obey. Place Your hand of blessing upon my household as we follow You every step of the way. In Jesus' Holy Name, Amen!"

Fathers give...Identity, Security, Provision, Protection & Direction

"Success God's Way!"

2 Chronicles 26:3-5

3 Uzziah was sixteen years old when he became king, and he reigned in Jerusalem fifty-two years. His mother's name was Jecoliah; she was from Jerusalem. 4 He did what was right in the eyes of the LORD, just as his father Amaziah had done. 5 He sought God during the days of Zechariah, who instructed him in the fear of God. As long as he sought the LORD, God gave him success.

"Young and inexperienced" is what everyone must have said about Uzziah. I guess we all have to start somewhere, but can you imagine being thrust into being a king at the age of 16? Oh yeah, he had a fairly good example in his father, but not a great one. The Bible says about Amaziah that, He did what was right in the eyes of the LORD, *but not wholeheartedly* (2 Chron. 25:2). That messes things up a bit doesn't it? His mentor did a lot of things right…*almost*!

Kind of sounds a lot like our lives in some ways doesn't it? We've had people who have led the way and shown us how "to do" and "not to do" life and leadership. For some of us, we've mainly had people over us who have shown us what "not to do" as they've led with mixed hearts and lives. What a shame! What is the answer? Verse 5 gives us a key that unlocks success and victory in any and every situation no matter what kind of examples we've had to follow. It simply says that *Uzziah sought God*. He didn't seek the counsel of men. He didn't look to every "King's Manual" he could lay his hands on…he sought God! Oh I'm sure he was surrounded with wise counselors and friends, but Uzziah recognized that if he was going to make it for the duration, he would need help from the only One who could give him real success.

As long as he sought the Lord, the Lord God prospered him. You see, success is not necessarily in the things we can accomplish, but it is in who we *are* at the end of our accomplishments. It seems so simple, and yet we miss it. If we would simply seek the Lord all the days of our lives, we would have success handed to us by God Almighty. God wants you to succeed and He has the perfect plan that will bring you to your greatest destiny…all you've got to do is seek first His Kingdom and His Righteousness, and all these *things* will be added to you. Psalm 18:35 says that the Lord is stooping down to make you great! Your job is simply to seek Him first! So…Happy Seeking!

"Lord, I want to acknowledge my need of You today. I realize that I can have no lasting success apart from You. Please give me a heart that continually seeks your wise counsel and wisdom Lord. I really do want to seek You first and sit at Your feet to get my marching orders. Help me Lord to never go my own way. Today I choose to fear You and You alone! Guide me every step of the way. I thank You for stooping down to make me great! You're an Awesome God and I praise you! Amen!"

"Why don't you go ahead and praise Him?"

Psalm 18:46

The LORD lives! Praise be to my Rock!
Exalted be God my Savior!

One of the things that I find hard to understand is why the Church of the Living God is so hesitant to praise the Lord with a loud voice. When it's time to praise the Lord it's like we put a muzzle over our mouths! We can whoop and holler and jump and dance when our team scores the big touchdown. We don't find it difficult to express ourselves in a ridiculous way when our kid scores a goal or hits a homerun. We celebrate so many things in life in such a way as to make a fool out of ourselves. Why then is it so hard for us to let loose in praise to the Lord of lords and the King of kings who is Alive...who has done so many amazing things for us...who is worthy and waiting to be praised?

The psalmist David realized that the Lord had brought him an amazing victory in his life. He sees the hand of God working on his behalf and he bursts forth with this verse of praise..."**The Lord lives! Praise be to my Rock! Exalted be God my Savior!**" Something broke out of the boundaries of David's inner being and began to shout forth...God is AMAZING and I *must* Praise Him! Something couldn't be contained in his heart any longer. He *had* to express himself because of his realization of what the Lord had done for him!

So what has God done for you? Isn't there *something* that you have a reason to praise Him for? I'm convinced that if we took the time to really think about all that the Lord has blessed us with, kept us from or poured out in our lives, we would find so much fuel for our fire of praise that it would never die out! We might even get a little radical in our praise to Him! You might just find us so overwhelmed by His goodness that we would be considered a "fan" or labeled a "fanatic"! Soccer moms beware…we are going to come unglued for God and may just put you to shame in your praise of your "little wonder". That's right! We can't help but praise Him!

"The Lord lives! I thank You Lord that You are alive and well! I see Your hand at work in my life. I'm overwhelmed at Your goodness and grace that You've shown me. You are an Awesome God! Praise be to my Rock! Praise to the One who is the strong and firm foundation of my life! The One who upholds me every day of my existence on this earth. The One who sustains me and gives me the power to live and gain wealth. The One who blesses me and my family and provides for my every need. Lord I am so grateful to You for all that You are to me. My lips praise You today! I exalt You and You alone. Exalted be God my Savior!"

"It's too loud in here!"

[8] When Asa heard these words and the prophecy of Azariah son of Oded the prophet, he took courage. He removed the detestable idols from the whole land of Judah and Benjamin and from the towns he had captured in the hills of Ephraim. He repaired the altar of the LORD that was in front of the portico of the LORD's temple.

[9] Then he assembled all Judah and Benjamin and the people from Ephraim, Manasseh and Simeon who had settled among them, for large numbers had come over to him from Israel when they saw that the LORD his God was with him.

[10] They assembled at Jerusalem in the third month of the fifteenth year of Asa's reign. [11] At that time they sacrificed to the LORD seven hundred head of cattle and seven thousand sheep and goats from the plunder they had brought back. [12] They entered into a covenant to seek the LORD, the God of their fathers, with all their heart and soul. [13] All who would not seek the LORD, the God of Israel, were to be put to death, whether small or great, man or woman. [14] They took an oath to the LORD with loud acclamation, with shouting and with trumpets and horns. [15] All Judah rejoiced about the oath because they had sworn it wholeheartedly. They sought God eagerly, and he was found by them. So the LORD gave them rest on every side.

When you start to get things right with God in your life…there is definitely a reason to rejoice! Earlier in this passage Azariah had said to Asa and the whole assembly, "The LORD is with you when you are with Him." What a thought! Get near God and He will be near you! That revelation gave Asa courage to remove what was wrong and rebuild what was right. You may need to tear some things out of your life to begin to get closer to God and see the results that you have longed for. You not only need to detach yourself from those things that are bent on destroying you, but you must repair the altar of the Lord in your life. When the people of God began to do just that, their hearts were moved to sacrifice to the Lord. When is the last time your heart pushed you to sacrifice something of significance to God? There's no time like the present!

I've said it many times…it's in the *doing* that the blessing comes. As they did things right, their hearts were turned. So many times we wait for a "feeling" before we are moved to do the right thing. The reality is that as we "do" the right thing, the "feelings" follow, along with the blessing! So what happened was that they began to do what God had asked them to do and they got excited! I wonder why it's acceptable to be loud anywhere but at church?

So many in church are concerned about how loud it is. I guess my biggest concern is how quiet it is! When we go after God wholeheartedly, with everything that is in us, it may just bring things up a few decibels! They shouted with loud acclamation, with trumpets and with horns. I'm a trumpet player and I'll be the first to tell you there is nothing quiet about a trumpet! When you get several thousand people shouting to God and add the trumpets and horns to the mix…brother it's gonna be loud!!! Maybe it's time to get things right in our lives and throw off our sanctimonious facades and just go ahead and let our voices be heard by God. Go ahead and take an oath before the Lord with your "outside voice"…I don't think it'll be too loud for Him!

"Lord, I seek You with all my heart today. I thank You that You promised to not hide from me. As I seek You eagerly, You will let me find You! Lord, give me the courage to remove the things from my life that shouldn't be there and to repair the altar of sacrifice. Today I open up my mouth with loud acclamation...with shouting and with my whole heart I declare that You are my God! I will seek You wholeheartedly! I will draw close to You! I will do what You have asked me to do! I will declare with my mouth and my actions that You are number one in my life! Thank you for the rest that brings to my soul. I rest in You today. Amen."

Private Victories Precede Public Victories!
Live your life Inside-Out!

"Stop Confronting us!"

Isaiah 30:9-11

[9] These are rebellious people, deceitful children,
children unwilling to listen to the LORD's instruction.

[10] They say to the seers,
"See no more visions!"
and to the prophets,
"Give us no more visions of what is right!
Tell us pleasant things,
prophesy illusions.

[11] Leave this way,
get off this path,
and stop confronting us
with the Holy One of Israel!"

You've probably met them in your church. They know what the Bible says because they've heard it preached for years. They've been around the "holy" most of their lives. They know right from wrong...even memorized scripture passages. The problem is that they just don't want to hear it any longer! They want to push their disobedience on everyone else so their conscience won't bother them any longer. Oh, they may not actually say it like this, but by their actions they are saying, "Stop confronting us with the Holy One! If the preacher would just stop confronting us with the truth then we could enjoy church! We like the fellowship, the friends, the business connections, the hang-out times...just stop confronting us with the truth! Tell us pleasant things...tickle our ears...make us feel good about how we're living. Why do you have to preach those things that cause conviction to come? STOP! Stop confronting us with the Holy One!"

It sounds all too current and up to date doesn't it? The scripture says that these are rebellious people, deceitful children, children unwilling to listen to the LORD's instruction. When you get to the point that you're unwilling to listen to God's instruction then you are living on very dangerous ground. We want the blessing of God, but don't want to walk the holy path of obedience to His Word. We want all the promises fulfilled in our lives, but aren't willing to live obediently as His children.

When is the last time you said…"Stop confronting me!"? Oh, it may not have been with your words, but by your actions you shouted it loudly. Someone speaks truth and you don't like it so you quit showing up to church for a while. You've got to let things cool off. The preacher talks about giving and you chafe at the teaching because it's "your money"! Someone mentions forgiving those who have wronged you and you bristle at the thought of letting the one who hurt you so badly somehow get off the hook! "Stop confronting me with the Holy One!"

May the Lord soften our hearts to the point that when we hear the truth, our immediate response is "Lord help me to follow Your ways!"

"Lord, I don't want to be like that. I don't want to be rebellious and unwilling to listen to Your instruction…whoever it comes through. Please soften my heart so that I will obey and follow the truth that You bring to me. Please continue to confront me so that I'll become all that You desire me to be. Your plans for me are amazing and I'll never get there without Your help. I want to follow Your ways and walk in Your truth! Make me more like YOU…the Holy One of Israel! Amen."

"Blueprints for Success!"

Isaiah 32:8

**⁸ But the noble man makes noble plans,
and by noble deeds he stands.**

You've heard it said, "If you don't plan to succeed, you are really planning to fail." Some people spend their lives just hoping that life will somehow work itself out…that they'll somehow end up with their preferred future. They don't really plan to fail, but by not planning to succeed they willingly send their lives in the total wrong direction. The dictionary defines "noble" as "having excellent moral character". Isaiah contrasts the "noble man" with a "fool". I'm sure you don't want to be a fool! Nobody sets out in life desiring to be a fool, but many end up there simply by default. They just don't make the right plans in life. I guess it's not really just about making plans either…it's about what you do with those plans that you've made. Planning is just the beginning…and a very important beginning I might add. But if you do nothing with your plans you might as well not have planned!

The scripture says that the noble man makes noble plans and by "noble deeds" he stands! It's what you **do** that makes all the difference in your life! James also talks about looking into the mirror of the Word of God and going away and not doing anything about what you've read. He basically says that when you do that it's like going out of the house without looking in the mirror! You see some people and think to yourself…poor guy…he doesn't own a mirror! If he owned a mirror he wouldn't have walked outside the door like that! It's the same with us if we don't do anything about what we know! If you want to be a noble person, then make some noble plans starting today and then do what needs to be done to bring about the results. When you do that, you will Stand!

"Lord, help me to become a noble person…a person after Your own heart. I don't want to be a fool. I want to follow You and Your plans for me wholeheartedly. Help me to become a doer of the Word and not a hearer only. I want everyone to know that I have a mirror and I use it! Thank You Lord for helping make me noble. Give me a planning and doing spirit as I trust in You! Amen."

Stay close to God in the Calm if you want Him close to you in the Storm

"Thank the Lord for Family!"

Psalm 68:5-6

**⁵ A father to the fatherless, a defender of widows,
is God in his holy dwelling.**

**⁶ God sets the lonely in families,
he leads forth the prisoners with singing;
but the rebellious live in a sun-scorched land.**

I grew up in a great family. I also grew up in a great church family! Isn't it interesting that the church is referred to as the family of God and so many don't even know what a functional family looks like? The church should be the greatest testimony of "family" on the face of the earth. God is all about helping and defending those who need a real Dad. So many fathers (and mothers) have abandoned their families in their pursuit of success, position or prosperity. They have left in their wake a lot of wounded and broken children and spouses who are hurting and lonely.

So what's the answer? God sets the lonely in families! The church is "a family" that is able to nurture and encourage the fatherless. We are called to be "Jesus with skin on" to everyone that crosses our path! Family sticks with you through thick and thin and pushes you to greatness…even if you'd rather just remain "status quo". As prisoners are led forth with singing they find themselves placed in a family by God Almighty. May we in the church surround those that God brings our way and provide all that we can to see them grow into their potential. Isn't that really what family is all about anyway?

Oh sure, there are some who will rebel and choose to live in a sun-scorched land, but when they come to their senses, the family is there waiting for them with open arms to welcome them back. There will be sounds of rejoicing as the party commences. Let's be the family God has called us to be! When we are, we reflect our Heavenly Father and His love for lost and hurting humanity.

"Lord give me Your heart for the fatherless and widows...for the prisoners who will soon be set free. Thank You for family! Help me to be the kind of family that shows Your loving kindness and compassion to those You bring my way. Give me all that I need to reach out to those in need. I really do want to be Jesus with skin on! Bless Your family throughout the earth and may Your Kingdom come, Your will be done here in me and in Your world wide family. Amen."

"Great Advice!"

Isaiah 7:1-9

4-9 ...'Be careful, keep calm and don't be afraid...If you do not stand firm in your faith, you will not stand at all.' "

Ahaz, King of Judah was being attacked by the enemy and hearing all kinds of reports of the armies that had allied with his enemies and he and his people were visibly shaken...as a tree is shaken by the wind. Sometimes we don't even have to see something. All we have to do is hear through the grapevine what *might* happen and we are shaken to our core! We hear the mention of cancer or recession or any number of things and we are quickly headed into a tailspin. Our faith is shaken by what should be a simple call to prayer and trust in our Lord!

The Lord told Isaiah to go tell Ahaz to "Be careful, keep calm and don't be afraid!" I think that is some great advice coming from the throne room of heaven! Be careful! Don't do anything stupid right now! Watch what you're doing. Use wisdom...don't do anything foolish in these moments. Stay calm...don't panic my friend! Let the peace of God surround you and calm your troubled mind and soul. Lean heavy on Him! And then, don't be afraid! Fear not! Someone has said that there are 366 "Fear not's" in the Bible...one for every day of the year plus one for leap year! I think the Lord wants us to trust Him and Him alone! It doesn't matter how big your situation is, God is bigger and He is able to do way beyond what you could ask or think! In verse 9 the Lord says, "If you do not stand firm in your faith, you will not stand at all." The key to us standing in the midst of any situation, no matter how huge, is to stand firm in the faith, not wavering. Our God is able to deliver us! He is greater! Greater is He who is in you than he that is in the world! Stand firm in your faith. Don't take your eyes off of the Savior…He is ABLE! So…Be Careful. Keep Calm. Don't be afraid. Stand firm in your faith. The Lord is with you!

"Lord I look to You and to You alone! I refuse to allow my circumstance to dictate how I will act. I will be careful. I will keep calm. I won't be afraid because I know that You are with me! I know that nothing can come my way unless You allow it. I also know that You work ALL things together for my good because I love You and I'm called according to Your purpose! Surround me with Your peace that goes way beyond my understanding. I choose today to stand firm in my faith…my faith in You and You alone! I love You Lord! Amen."

"Whose money is it anyway?"

Psalm 54:6-7

[6] I will sacrifice a freewill offering to you;
I will praise your name, O LORD,
for it is good.

[7] For he has delivered me from all my troubles,
and my eyes have looked in triumph on my foes.

1 Chronicles 29:6-12

[6] Then the leaders of families, the officers of the tribes of Israel, the commanders of thousands and commanders of hundreds, and the officials in charge of the king's work gave willingly. [7] They gave toward the work on the temple of God...[9] The people rejoiced at the willing response of their leaders, for they had given freely and wholeheartedly to the LORD. David the king also rejoiced greatly. [10] David praised the LORD in the presence of the whole assembly, saying,
"Praise be to you, O LORD,
God of our father Israel,
from everlasting to everlasting.

[11] Yours, O LORD, is the greatness and the power
and the glory and the majesty and the splendor,
for everything in heaven and earth is yours.
Yours, O LORD, is the kingdom;
you are exalted as head over all.

[12] Wealth and honor come from you;
you are the ruler of all things.
In your hands are strength and power
to exalt and give strength to all.

When it comes to talking about giving money in the church…everyone cringes! I'm not sure why we are so uptight about money, but the fact remains that only a handful of believers tithe. The latest polls show that only a mere 4% of Christians give at least 10% of their income to the Lord's work. Are you serious???!!!!???? Who gave you the ability that you have? Who gave you breath this morning? Who allows you to live one more moment so you can go to work and collect that paycheck? Whose money is it anyway? If we really thought it through we would come to the conclusion that David did…Everything in heaven and earth is Yours, O LORD! Wealth and honor come from You!

Not one of us is a self-made man or woman. We are only able to do what we do by the grace of God. If He wanted to, He could snatch your life away from you at any moment. Praise God He doesn't! We, like David, have an opportunity to sacrifice a freewill offering to the Lord for what He has done in our lives. When David and the leaders gave freely and wholeheartedly to the Lord it was a time of great celebration! Every need was met and God's kingdom was established. Oh that we would have the same heart as David did. Oh that we would have hearts that give freely to the Lord's work…not by coercion or prodding, but willingly, freely and wholeheartedly giving, realizing that it's all His in the first place. He just lets me manage it. May I manage what He's blessed me with well! May I willingly give the firstfruits of all He blesses me with to Him so I can fully trust Him to take care of the rest! He is an Awesome God and deserves our all!

"Lord I give You all of me today…even my money. It's really all Yours anyway! I acknowledge that You are the One who owns it all and You have allowed me to steward a portion of Your wealth. Wealth and honor come from You and I thank You that You are caring for me. Help me

to steward well. Give me a willing, giving, generous heart oh Lord. Thank You for all that You've blessed me with. I honor You with all that I am! Amen."

TRIUMPH is made up of two words...

TRY & UMPH!

"Who's walking with you?"

Isaiah 49:25

**[25] But this is what the LORD says:
"Yes, captives will be taken from warriors,
and plunder retrieved from the fierce;
I will contend with those who contend with you,
and your children I will save.**

There's nothing like someone standing up for you or your kids. I remember walking to the bus stop one morning to handle a "situation" with our little kindergartner Elijah. He wore glasses and was just a little tyke. He had come home one day with broken glasses and I asked him what had happened. He proceeded to tell me that the big kids on the bus would pull his glasses off everyday and toss them around. "What?" I said, "You've got to be kidding me!" And then he said, "Dad, I don't want to ride the bus anymore." I looked him in the eyes and said, "Elijah, tomorrow I'm going to the bus stop with you and we're going to have a chat with the bus folk!" He said, "You'd do that Dad?" "You bet! Tomorrow, I'm going with you!" I replied. Elijah used to go to the bus stop with his shoulders slouched and his head down, but the next day was different. He put his little hand in my hand and started to strut as if to say…"We're going to the bus!" **It matters who is walking with you!!!** We got to the bus stop and I had a little chat with everyone on the bus including the bus driver. Elijah never had another problem on that bus. I'll say it again…it matters who's walking with you!

When the LORD says that He will contend with those who contend with you, you've got the God of the universe walking with you! The One who spoke the world into existence is on your side and is standing against your enemies! When the enemy attacks, God says He will contend with them and save your kids as well. Maybe you need God to intervene in your kids lives. You need Him to rescue them from the hand of the enemy…they've been captive way too long! His promise is not just for you but for your children too. What a deal! What an awesome God! What a strong promise from our Heavenly Father! I stand on that today!

"Lord I thank You that You are contending with those who contend with me. I don't have to fight for myself because You are fighting for me! If God is for me then who can be against me! I will stand today in that truth and put my hand in Your hand. I will walk confidently, knowing that You are with me. Even that which the enemy has taken from me will be taken back by You no matter how fierce the enemy is. You will set the captives free and will save my children! You are my Awesome God and I praise You today as I walk hand in hand with You! Amen!"

"Tongue Training 101"

Isaiah 50:4-5

[4] The Sovereign LORD has given me an instructed
tongue,
to know the word that sustains the weary.
He wakens me morning by morning,
wakens my ear to listen like one being taught.

[5] The Sovereign LORD has opened my ears,
and I have not been rebellious;
I have not drawn back.

Can you imagine how much trouble that little muscle in your mouth has caused you? It's so unruly! Have you ever heard yourself say something and then thought, "Why did I say that? Where did that come from?" We've all done it and lived with regrets from what we've allowed to come out of our mouths. This scripture has become a prayer and a declaration that I speak on a regular basis. "The Sovereign LORD has given me an instructed tongue, to know the word that sustains the weary." If I'll listen to what He is speaking to me everyday…if I haven't been rebellious and closed my ears to His words, then I can expect Him to fill my mouth with a sustaining word for someone else!

What could happen in your life if every time you spoke to someone, your words were like a cool drink of water in a dry and weary land? What if you spoke with an instructed tongue the words that brought life to those who were dying? What if your words had sustaining power that lifted the weary soul to new heights? What if you could say just the right thing to everyone you meet? I believe it's possible and that God actually wants to use us in such a way! First of all I have to listen every morning to what He is speaking to me. I must tune my ear in to heaven.

If I want an "instructed tongue"…a tongue that is trained to say the right things at the right time then I've got to do my part in sitting in His classroom and hearing His voice. When I do my part…God does His part…speaking through me His life-giving words!

"Lord I choose today to sit at Your feet and learn of You. I ask You to instruct my tongue as I yield it to Your purposes. Bring someone across my path today who needs a sustaining word and give me the courage to speak it. May my ears be attentive to Your powerful, healing and instructing voice today. Thank You for using me to bring a slice of heaven to earth! Amen."

"Good, Better, Best!"

Isaiah 48:17

**[17] This is what the LORD says—
your Redeemer, the Holy One of Israel:
"I am the LORD your God,
who teaches you what is best for you,
who directs you in the way you should go.**

Have you ever had the feeling that you knew better than your instructor? Oh they had the degree on the wall, but you had plenty of experience! Your attitude pretty much kept you from learning anything from them. I wonder if we get into the same issue with the Lord. Sometimes our posture is one of a know-it-all. We act like we don't need God to tell us anything. We don't read His Word. We don't spend any time listening in prayer to His still small voice. We go headlong in our own way hoping to come to a preferred outcome, not knowing that if we would just take some time to hear Him, we might just be better off for it! God says that He teaches us what is BEST for us! My Grandma Briney used to say, "Good, better, best. Never let it rest, till your good becomes your better and your better is your BEST!"

I think we all would like the Best in life! No one sets out in life striving for mediocrity. I've never heard anyone say that their dream in life is to go down the wrong path, make lots of mistakes and having a boring, nondescript, mediocre life! That's just not our goal, yet somehow we get duped into thinking that we can have the best in life by doing our own thing. If we would just follow the Lord and His amazing ways, we would learn from Him what is best for us! He wants to teach us the best way. He wants to direct us in the best path. His desire is that we would simply follow Him down the pathway of the plans He has for us…the Best possible plans! He designed us for a purpose and knows best how we work. He has redeemed us and put us back on the best possible pathway for our preferred future if only we will listen and obey His guidance. He really does want what's best for you. Why don't you go ahead and follow Him?

"Lord I really want the best that You have for me. I'm not sure why I seem to always want to go my own way and do my own thing. Help me to lay down my pride and learn from You, The Master of the universe! Thank You for caring so much about me that You paid the price to redeem me. Thank You for teaching me what is best for me and for directing me in the way that I should go. Guide me every single day of my life to Your preferred future for me. I trust in You! Amen."

"Trust & Obey"

Isaiah 50:10-11

[10] **Who among you fears the LORD**
and obeys the word of his servant?
Let him who walks in the dark,
who has no light,
trust in the name of the LORD
and rely on his God.

[11] **But now, all you who light fires**
and provide yourselves with flaming torches,
go, walk in the light of your fires
and of the torches you have set ablaze.
This is what you shall receive from my hand:
You will lie down in torment.

The old song goes something like this…"Trust and Obey. For there's no other way. To be happy in Jesus. Than to trust and obey." The word of the Lord asked the question, "Who among you fears the Lord and obeys the word of His servant?" The following sentence brings out the need to trust and rely on God. The following verse basically says that if you don't trust God and you do your own thing…good luck! All you've got is all you've got! If you want to walk through the dark with only what you can come up with then you will find yourself in a real mess. But if you lean on the Lord and His wisdom…follow His ways…trust and rely on Him…you'll have all that God has!

I've been around the church for over 50 years and one thing I've come to know…humble, helpless people win with God! The reality is that God resists those who are proud. That means that when you are proud you actually have the God of the universe working against you! He is resisting you! Who wants that? No one who has much sense does! God does resist the proud, but He gives grace to the humble. When you humble yourself under the mighty hand of God and trust in

Him and His wisdom, you get all that He is, working in your behalf! Nothing quite like that! So why not trust and obey Him today…there's definitely no better way to be happy than that!

"Lord help me today. I really do need You! I'm tired of doing my own thing…I need Your light to illuminate my path. I put my whole trust and hope in You today. I rely on You and know that You won't ever let me down. You want what is best for me! I'm not going to strike out in the dark on my own with my own abilities…I need You. I need Your wisdom and guidance today. Help me as I navigate today. Lead me by Your Word…Your voice to me. I trust in You! Amen."

"No weapon stands a chance!"

Isaiah 54:17

**[17] no weapon forged against you will prevail,
and you will refute every tongue that accuses you.
This is the heritage of the servants of the LORD,
and this is their vindication from me,"
declares the LORD.**

You probably know by now that the enemy of your soul has many weapons. He has aimed his destructive missiles at you more than once in your Christian journey I'm sure. Discouragement, threats, loneliness, sexual temptation, vicious words, destructive thoughts and the list goes on and on! It can seem like a never ending assault on your faith as you walk this narrow road. I've got good news for you today from the very mouth of Almighty God…the Creator of the universe…the One who gives life to the dead! He says, "No weapon forged against you will prevail!" No weapon that comes against you even has a chance! And He goes on to say, "You will refute every tongue that accuses you!" You have the power in your mouth to put the enemy in his place…every time! This is your heritage as a servant of the Lord! This is your HERITAGE…your legal right as a child of God! You were born into that ability when you became a child of the living God! Don't just sit there…declare with your mouth what God says about you! Declare with your mouth the victory that is yours! Speak the Word of God with boldness! The enemy's got nothing that you can't refute with the Word of God. Go ahead and take your stand! God will vindicate you. God will fight for you. Your Heavenly Father is giving you the ability to destroy every weapon that comes your way! Stand up…open up your mouth and speak the Word of God with all boldness! "No weapon forged against me will prevail!"

"I thank You Lord today for the ability that You have given me. I thank You that no weapon that comes my way will be able to penetrate my life. You have given me the ability to speak up with the power of Your Words. You will fill my mouth with the Word of the Living God...the words that I need to refute every tongue that accuses me. Thank You for such an incredible heritage! I'm so glad to be a part of Your amazing family! I take my stand today against every onslaught of the enemy...in Jesus' Name! Amen!"

"The Blessing of a man who fears the Lord!"

Psalm 112

[1] Praise the LORD.
Blessed is the man who fears the LORD,
who finds great delight in his commands.

[2] His children will be mighty in the land;
the generation of the upright will be blessed.

[3] Wealth and riches are in his house,
and his righteousness endures forever.

[4] Even in darkness light dawns for the upright,
for the gracious and compassionate and righteous
man.

[5] Good will come to him who is generous and lends
freely,
who conducts his affairs with justice.

[6] Surely he will never be shaken;
a righteous man will be remembered forever.

[7] He will have no fear of bad news;
his heart is steadfast, trusting in the LORD.

[8] His heart is secure, he will have no fear;
in the end he will look in triumph on his foes.

[9] He has scattered abroad his gifts to the poor,
his righteousness endures forever;
his horn will be lifted high in honor.

**¹⁰ The wicked man will see and be vexed,
he will gnash his teeth and waste away;
the longings of the wicked will come to nothing.**

People have said to me, "I wish I had a family like yours!" My response to many of them is, "No you don't...because it's too much work!" If you do the hard work that we've done then you can have the same blessing we have. It's just that simple. It seems that so many just want the blessing without the doing! The Psalmist declares that the man who fears the Lord and follows His commands will receive amazing blessings.

One of the benefits of fearing the Lord and following His ways is that your children will be mighty in the land. They will grow and mature into mighty leaders in a land of followers. They will have God's hand of favor on their lives. It flows to the next generation of those who fear the Lord. Wealth and riches will be in your house. Oh they might not be the monetary riches you're thinking about, but when your family is living for God and following His ways, you are wealthy indeed! I've had conversations with very wealthy individuals who said they would give all the money they've acquired to have the family that I've been blessed with.

When you follow God and His ways you are wealthy beyond what this world can offer. Even when it's the darkest in your life, God will turn the lights on for you so that you can see your way through every storm & tempest. His Word is a lamp to your feet and a light to your path. As you are generous (that Godly attribute that lets people know you really are His kid) you will never be shaken. The headlines that cause everyone else to quake with fear won't bother you a bit...because you trust in the Lord! No Fear! You've done what God has asked of you and so you and your children will receive the amazing benefits! What a way to go! Praise the Lord!

"Lord my desire is to follow You and Your ways. My only fear is You! I put my trust and hope in You and thank You for the amazing benefits that flow my way. I stand secure when everyone and everything around me is quaking because I have made You my Rock, my God, my Lord. Teach me Your ways and give me the strength to follow so that my children will be mighty in the land! May their blessing flow to the next generation of those who fear You! I praise You Almighty God! Amen."

"Hold me Daddy!"

Isaiah 46:3-4

[3] **"Listen to me, O house of Jacob,
all you who remain of the house of Israel,
you whom I have upheld since you were conceived,
and have carried since your birth.**

[4] **Even to your old age and gray hairs
I am he, I am he who will sustain you.
I have made you and I will carry you;
I will sustain you and I will rescue you.**

I'm much older now than when I first wrote this scripture down in my journal and claimed it as a promise to me from God. My hair is definitely gray and I'm quickly approaching "old age"! God says…Listen to Me! I was around before you were even a twinkle in your father's eye and I am the one who has carried you since you finally showed up on this earth. Do you think I would forget you? Are you really concerned that I won't take care of my own? I am the One who will sustain you. I have made you and I will carry you!

As a father myself, I spent many years carrying my kids around. When my daughter Alexsondra came into this world you would have thought that she didn't have any legs…she always wanted me to carry her. "Hold me Daddy" was her constant mantra. I carried her all over the place until I just wasn't physically able to do it any more. I've got good news for you today. God will always be able to carry you! He will never tire of sustaining and rescuing you! He is a Father who will take care of your every need as long as you live…and then beyond that into eternity! There are so many times in my life when Father God has upheld me and sustained me when I couldn't make it on my own. I've been carried, sustained and rescued by Him more times than I even know. What an awesome God! He'll be there for you as well…just cry out, "Hold me Daddy!", and feel His strong arms pick you up and lift you high above it all…no matter how old you are.

"Lord I really do need You to carry me today. I need Your strong arms to surround me and pick me up. I'm old enough now to know when I need Your helping hand and so I cry out to You today…Hold me Daddy! I need You today and always! Thank You for Your sustaining power. Thank You for rescuing me even when I don't recognize You in the midst of everything. Thank You for upholding me today and forever! Amen."

"What are you worth?"

Ephesians 4:1
[1]As a prisoner for the Lord, then, I urge you to live a life worthy of the calling you have received.

What comes to mind when you say the word "worthy"? Do you think of someone who has done everything right in their life and so they are worthy of whatever? Does a person come to mind who was born into a "special" family and gets special privileges? The dictionary defines worthy as "fully deserving something, morally upright, good and deserving respect, having good qualities, etc." Who can live up to that? I think sometimes we may feel totally opposite…inadequate and unworthy. If you have feelings of inadequacy how in the world are you supposed to live a life worthy of the calling you've received from God?

I've heard it said that *the worth of an object is what someone is willing to pay for it*! If that is the case then you are worth the price of God's Son, Jesus Christ. God thinks you are worth His Son's life! He paid the highest price for you! All He's asking you to do is to live a life worthy of that! When you know what something is worth you treat it with greater respect. You don't wear a $2000 suit to wallow in the mud! You wouldn't drive a $200,000 sports car through an off-road course…its worth too much! When I fully understand the price that God has paid for me, it elevates my understanding of who I am. I can't live like I used to…I'm worth too much! I can't get dirty with those things again…I'm worth too much! I don't want to go there anymore, say those things anymore, be like that anymore…I'm worth way too much! God has set me apart for greatness and I will walk worthy of the calling He has placed on my life!

"Lord help me to understand my worth in You. My desire is to live my life in such a way that it is worthy of the calling You have placed on my life. I realize I can't do that without Your help and so I ask You to help me today! Keep my worth in You ever before my eyes so that I will stay pure and holy in Your sight. Lead me in the way that I should go today and thank You for making me worthy! Lord I find my worth in You! I love You and will follow You all the days of my life! Amen."

"He's an Awesome God!"

Psalm 68:28

**28 Summon your power, O God;
show us your strength, O God, as you have done
before.**

What a bold statement! Summon Your power, O God; show us Your strength, O God, as You have done before! When is the last time you spoke with that kind of boldness? When is the last time you called upon God Almighty to do what only He can do? Someone has said, "We must restore fierceness to our times of prayer!" I believe it's high time we began to make a strong declaration …O God we need to see Your power and strength today as we have seen before. We've got to have You show up here…now!

How long has it been since you have seen God's power displayed? When is the last time you saw His strength with your own eyes. David had seen God's power in the past, and he knew that this situation was hopeless unless the power of God was unleashed once again. I need the power of God evident in my life like it was in days gone by.

My Grandpa Hollis was a man of great faith and I used to love to go to his garage and see all the canes, crutches and wheel chairs hanging on the walls. Each one had a story of the awesome power of God that had brought healing to so many. Grandpa prayed for 3 people, that we know of who were raised from the dead! He was a man who just believed that if God said it then He meant it and Grandpa was going to pray and believe that it would happen! Oh that we would have that kind of faith today! Without God those things were impossible. But God is all powerful! I wonder if we really believe that.

My prayer and bold confession today is...Summon Your power, O God; show us Your strength, O God, as You have done before! I don't want to just hear about Your power...I want to experience it and see it today!

"It's true Lord...I don't want to just hear about Your power...I want to see it in my life! I need to experience the power that comes only from You. So I'm asking You today to show me Your strength, O God. Even if I've never seen it before...I've read about it in Your Word. Let me see Your power and strength displayed so that all will see and know that You are God! I need You to invade my situation and do what no one else can do...be God! I invite You to summon Your power and show me Your strength, O God...as You have done before! Thank You! I'm so grateful. Amen."

"I will follow You!"

Isaiah 48:17-19

[17] This is what the LORD says—
your Redeemer, the Holy One of Israel:
"I am the LORD your God,
who teaches you what is best for you,
who directs you in the way you should go.

[18] If only you had paid attention to my commands,
your peace would have been like a river,
your righteousness like the waves of the sea.

[19] Your descendants would have been like the sand,
your children like its numberless grains;
their name would never be cut off
nor destroyed from before me."

You may remember when you were young and thought that your parents were so out of date and didn't have a clue! They just didn't know anything! Their only goal was to make your life miserable. And then you grew up and somehow they became smarter and wiser than you could even comprehend! You may have even paid a very high price for not listening to their wise counsel and going your own stubborn way. I wonder if we treat God the same way. We think we know it all. We are convinced that our way is the best way...our way is the most fulfilling way. God doesn't know anything! He's so out of date! Oh we may not say it with our words, but our actions are all about it.

God desires to teach us what is best for us. He wants to direct us in the way that we should go...the way that will bring us everything we've ever longed for. It's a way that brings such peace, contentment and righteousness (being in right standing with Him…nothing quite like that!). His way fulfills our every longing. It holds the blessings that we have searched for and couldn't find on our own pathway. Oh that we would learn our lessons. Oh that we would surrender our stubborn wills to the One who wants the best for us…the One who is willing to lead and guide us to our desired haven if we would only listen and follow. I know our human tendency is to strike out on our own and do our own thing. The cost is very high though. Sin will always take you farther than you wanted to go. It will make you stay longer than you ever planned on staying. And sin will make you pay more than you ever dreamed you'd have to pay! Why not just pay attention to His commands and follow His ways today. I have a very strong feeling that if you do, you will be blessed beyond your ability to contain it!

"Oh Lord help me to always follow Your ways and listen to Your voice. I know deep down in my heart that You want what is best for me. I am learning that Your ways are so much better for me than my own ways and plans. Give me a listening ear and an obedient heart to follow You all the days of my life. I don't want to be rebellious. Today I will pay attention! I will receive Your amazing blessings because of it! I will follow You! Amen."

"What's that on Your hand?"

Isaiah 49:13-16

[13] Shout for joy, O heavens;
rejoice, O earth;
burst into song, O mountains!
For the LORD comforts his people
and will have compassion on his afflicted ones.

[14] But Zion said, "The LORD has forsaken me,
the Lord has forgotten me."

[15] "Can a mother forget the baby at her breast
and have no compassion on the child she has borne?
Though she may forget,
I will not forget you!

[16] See, I have engraved you on the palms of my hands;
your walls are ever before me.

Have you ever felt abandoned and forsaken? It seemed like everyone, including God, had forgotten you and left you to somehow make it on your own. It's in those moments that we start throwing the biggest pity party in the world. No one cares! Not even God! At least that's how we feel. I know I've been there a few times in my life and asked some big questions. Let me tell you from experience…God knows what you're going through and He is ever mindful of you. He responds by asking a question of us. "Can a mother forget and have no compassion for the baby she has borne?" And even if she can forget, God says, "I WILL NOT FORGET YOU!" The most amazing thing to me is the statement that He follows with…"See, I have engraved you on the palms of my hands."

I don't know if you're like me, but when I need to really remember something I'll write it on my hand. That way anytime I look at my hand I'm reminded of what it is I need to think about. Comprehend this…that the God of the universe has written your name on the palms of His hands! He's not only written your name, but *engraved it* so it will never wash off! God is constantly thinking about you. He knows exactly where you are and what you're going through. He has not forsaken you! He can't forget you…you are engraved on the palms of His hands! What a thought! What an amazing God!

"Lord thank You for constantly thinking about me. Thank You that You never forget me and are always surrounding me with Your comfort and compassion. I confess that there are moments when I doubt You and feel like You've forgotten and forsaken me. I'm sorry for that. Your Word reassures me that I'm engraved on the palms of Your hands. Wow! That is almost too much to take in, but I thank You for that promise. You will not forget me! I'm overwhelmed by Your amazing love. I'm shouting for joy today! Amen."

"Who's your Daddy?"

Isaiah 65:11-15

[11] "But as for you who forsake the LORD
and forget my holy mountain,
who spread a table for Fortune
and fill bowls of mixed wine for Destiny,

[12] I will destine you for the sword,
and you will all bend down for the slaughter;
for I called but you did not answer,
I spoke but you did not listen.
You did evil in my sight
and chose what displeases me."

[13] Therefore this is what the Sovereign LORD says:
"My servants will eat,
but you will go hungry;
my servants will drink,
but you will go thirsty;
my servants will rejoice,
but you will be put to shame.

[14] My servants will sing
out of the joy of their hearts,
but you will cry out
from anguish of heart
and wail in brokenness of spirit.

[15] You will leave your name
to my chosen ones as a curse;
the Sovereign LORD will put you to death,
but to his servants he will give another name.

Everyone seems to be going after "their thing" these days. Working hard to build a nest egg for retirement. Keeping up with the Jones'. Trying to find their fortune. Reaching out in so many different ways for their destiny. We search and search for meaning in this life and can't seem to quite get there. Unless of course we have given our whole hearts to the Lord and follow His plan. That changes everything! The Lord is saying that if you forget Him and run after everything else, then you are missing the whole point.

We seem to go after everything we think will bring us fulfillment and happiness and forsake the only One who can bring it all to pass! When we spread a table for Fortune and wine and dine Destiny and forget the God who holds it all in His hands, we are making a huge mistake! God says, seek Me first and you will eat, drink, rejoice and sing. You will find your fortune and your destiny will be secure. Don't get so blinded by Fortune and Destiny that you can't see clearly. It's so easy to do in a world that pushes that in our faces every day.

The Sovereign Lord is your answer to the greatest destiny you could ever dream of! His fortunes don't fade away...they can't be stolen or depleted! Your earthly retirement may fade with the ebb and flow of Wall Street and the economy, but God's retirement package is amazing...and it's FOREVER! Don't forsake the Lord and chase after things that will fade away. Don't forget the One who can bless you beyond your wildest dreams. Choose Life!

"Lord, I choose life today. I choose You and Your ways. There are so many times that I lose sight of what's really important, but today I realign myself with You and Your plan for me. You are my God and You want what is best for me. Thank You for being my Heavenly Father...the One who has an amazing plan for my life. I choose today what pleases You and I know I'll be blessed in the process! Amen."

"Don't be senseless!"

Jeremiah 10:21

**21 The shepherds are senseless
and do not inquire of the LORD;
so they do not prosper
and all their flock is scattered.**

Can you imagine being put in charge of taking care of
something and not checking with the owner on how to care for
it? Or maybe being a babysitter and not asking the mother
what needs to be done or not even listening to the father's
instructions as he tries to explain what the baby will need?
How absurd would that be? It's quite the same as a shepherd
or pastor not inquiring of the Lord about His flock! The Lord
says to Jeremiah that those kinds of shepherds are
senseless! How hard would it be to inquire of the Lord to see
what He says? If we would only realize that God Almighty
knows best and desires to bless His flock...all He wants us to
do is inquire of Him and follow His instructions! The result of
senseless shepherds is that they do not prosper.

 How sad to think that so many pastors/shepherds have the
ability to prosper and lead the flock of God, but they just won't
inquire of God and listen to His directives. Their flock is
scattered and have become vulnerable to the ravenous
wolves that are just waiting to pick them off one by one. It's
not just pastors either. Maybe you have a place of leadership
in your family or at your job. Could it be that God knows
exactly what your sheep need? Is it possible that He wants to
prosper your flock and lead you and them to green pastures?
Why not inquire of the Lord today and listen to His voice
guiding and directing you? Trust me; your sheep will be glad
you did!

"Lord I'm tuning my ear in to hear Your voice today. I'm asking You to lead and guide me as I lead and guide those You've placed in my care. I need Your help. I need Your guidance and wisdom. I want my flock to prosper and not be scattered. Please help me Lord. I humble myself before You today and seek Your face. You are so gracious to guide me in the ways of truth and life! Thank You Lord for the blessings that will flow as I listen to You! Amen."

"Promotion comes from the Lord"

Psalm 78:70-72

[70] He chose David his servant
and took him from the sheep pens;

[71] from tending the sheep he brought him
to be the shepherd of his people Jacob,
of Israel his inheritance.

[72] And David shepherded them with integrity of heart;
with skillful hands he led them.

I wonder if David realized when he was shepherding sheep out in the lonely fields that this was simply training for his true calling in life. Do you think he had any idea that someday he would be shepherding God's flock? I kind of doubt it. I think that he was just loving God with all his heart and doing whatever his hand found to do…with excellence…realizing that he was working for the Lord, not men. David just did what was in his heart to do and that's why God chose him to lead His people. God looked over the face of the then known world and searched for someone who could handle the job of leading His chosen ones. If we could only realize that the seemingly mundane, little, often unnoticed things we are doing right now are so very, very important. Our Heavenly Father is watching and in a moments notice is able to promote us from the sheep pen to the palace! God isn't going to promote someone who is lazy and just looking to get ahead. David had integrity of heart and used the skills that he had learned the hard way to lead in his new position…a position given by God! Maybe, just maybe the Lord is waiting for your skills to be honed and your heart to get ready for your new assignment!

"Lord prepare me for whatever You have planned for me. Prepare my heart. Let integrity be the benchmark of my life. Help me Lord always to realize that I'm not working for my boss or for this company or these people…I'm working wholeheartedly for You…and You are watching carefully. You will promote in due time. You will place me where You want me to be. I will do what I can do and will rely on You to do the rest! I love You Lord! Amen!"

"Whose word is it?"

Jeremiah 23:29-30

[29] **"Is not my word like fire," declares the LORD, "and like a hammer that breaks a rock in pieces? [30] "Therefore," declares the LORD, "I am against the prophets who steal from one another words supposedly from me.**

Seems as though the prophets were not seeking the Lord for a fresh word from Him. It looks like they were waiting to hear what another prophet would say and would just repeat his words as a word from the Lord. How sad a time that was. I wonder if we're living in the same kind of moment today? I remember when we were traveling as a family ministry and 9/11 happened. We ministered in a church that next Sunday as usual, but the pastor said he needed to share a message and asked if we would just sing. We totally understood that the shepherd needed to bring a timely word of comfort to his flock from God. It was a good message…a message that seemed well thought out. The next Sunday we were at our next assignment and I found a copy of the pastor's message from the past Sunday in one of the chairs as I was praying in the sanctuary. It was the exact same message…the fill-in-the-blank notes were exactly the same…word for word!!!! I couldn't believe my eyes! Somehow I had believed that men of God turned to the Word of God for a word from God. Needless to say I was very disappointed and wondered if this is what the Lord was referring to. Oh, I read and study and have taken quotes and ideas from many different sources, but when we need a word from the Lord…we need a word from the LORD! I believe God wants to give you a fresh word from Him that is found in His Word…a word that is like fire…a word that is like a hammer and has the power to break a rock in pieces! That's what we need! I don't ever want the Lord to be against me and neither do you!

"Lord I humble myself before You today and I ask for Your forgiveness for the times that I've stolen words from someone else and passed them off as a word from You. I turn to Your Word today to find a fresh word to share with those in need...a word that burns up the dross and hammers those hard things and breaks them into pieces...a powerful word from You alone! Thank You for speaking to me a fresh word today. I honor You! Amen."

"It's not just about you!"

1 Timothy 4:16

[16]Watch your life and doctrine closely. Persevere in them, because if you do, you will save both yourself and your hearers.

Paul the apostle loved his son in the faith. Timothy was dear to him and he spent much time guiding him in the ways of life. He gave him much advice with the hope that Timothy would become the man of God that he was destined to be. I don't know if anyone has cared enough about you to pour that kind of love and instruction into you, but it is a treasure that pays big dividends. Maybe you have the opportunity to mentor and encourage a younger person in the faith. Take advantage of every moment and give instruction that will bring life to them. Paul's advice here is not just good advice…it is the wisdom of God. Watch your life and your doctrine closely. It really does matter what you believe! Your beliefs create your behaviors. What you believe has a huge impact on what you do! You need to believe right so that you live right!

Then there is that word "persevere". Perseverance simply means *determined continuation*…it has a connotation that something is going to come against you and you will have to *push on through* to get to your desired end. If you persevere in your godly life and doctrine then you will not only save yourself but you will save those who are listening to you and following you. I know way too many leaders who have stumbled in their walk with the Lord and have brought severe ruin to themselves, their families and to so many who were listening intently to their message. They became so self-absorbed that they really didn't care what happened to those who were following them. What a tragedy!

Watch your life closely my friend! Watch your doctrine closely. If you will push on through the tough times then you will be saved and so will those who are following and listening to you. It really is about more than just you!

"O Lord please give me eyes to see when I'm heading in the wrong direction. Grant me the perseverance I need to stay on the straight and narrow pathway...the path that leads to life! I know that there are those who are following me and I need to lead well. May my life be a testimony of godliness and of purity. I need Your help today. Guide me by Your Holy Spirit into all truth. I will persevere and will receive the crown of life! Thank You Lord! Amen."

"A Curse?"

Jeremiah 48:10

[10] "A curse on him who is lax in doing the LORD's work!..."

I think the first time I remember reading this scripture I was pretty young in ministry. I thought it was a very harsh statement. Calling down a curse on someone who is in the Lord's work seems harsh doesn't it? Come on...there are others who may deserve a curse, but surely not the Lord's workers! The older I've gotten and the more I've been around, I'm not so convinced it's all that harsh anymore. If you've been called to do the Lord's work then you should be one of the hardest working people on the planet! Your work is not just for the here and now...it's eternal stuff we're talking about! We're talking life and death here! Eternal life and death!

If God has asked you to do something and you don't do it, you are calling down a curse on your own head. Did I really say that? Maybe it's just an Old Testament thing, but I think the principle is pretty sound. The apostle Paul said in the New Testament that whatever your hand finds to do you should work at it with all your might...realizing that you're working for the Lord, not for men! I've met way too many people in the Lord's work who are just out to collect a paycheck or for the prestige and position. If you're in the Lord's work...and aren't we all...then let's get up and get moving! This is no game my friend. Someone's life hangs in the balance!

"Lord I come to You today needing Your help in all I do. I don't want to be lazy or half-hearted in my work for You.

Give me eyes to see the harvest that is before me and the strength to do all that You've called me to do. I know there are so many lives hanging in the balance between life and death. Help me to stand in the gap on their behalf. Give me all that I need to reach them with Your love. I love You Lord! Amen."

Wanted: Chapped Eyes

"No way! Not today!"

Psalm 118:17

**[17] I will not die but live,
and will proclaim what the LORD has done.**

I don't know if you've ever been close to death or know of anyone who has but it is definitely a reality check. It's a time when you really find out what you're made of. You discover who you really put your trust in. I was much younger then and thought that I was invincible. I was a co-pastor of a church and a youth pastor of a thriving youth ministry when I got so sick I couldn't even get off the couch to get into our bed. After much testing and blood work it was discovered that I had contracted Hepatitis B and Mononucleosis at the same time. I shelved everything I was doing, including a city-wide high school assembly outreach program we had scheduled for over a year, and went to bed. It was a very trying time in my young life. There were times that I was so sick that I thought I really might die…I had never been so sick in my entire life. I was out of commission for 6 weeks…I could hardly move. I looked awful and felt even worse.

This scripture became my mantra…I will not die but live, and will proclaim what the LORD has done! No way! Not today! I've got work to do for the Kingdom of God! I eventually got my strength back and picked my ministry back up…with more wisdom and parameters for living. I didn't die…but I am still proclaiming what the Lord has done! He has intervened in my life in so many ways since then and I am living to proclaim His goodness. I don't know what you're going through today, but God does and He wants to give you life…a life that is a testimony of His grace and greatness. Why not declare today…I will not die…but live! And I will proclaim what the LORD has done!

"Lord I thank You for Your life giving power today. You are the healer of my body. You are the healer of my soul. I boldly proclaim today that I will not die...but I will live! I will live and I will tell of Your greatness! I will proclaim what You have done for me...things too great to contain! Thank You for Your life-giving power that flows to me and through me. Let it flow to everyone I come in contact with today in the name of our Lord Jesus Christ! Amen."

"I get it now!"

Proverbs 28:5

**⁵ Evil men do not understand justice,
but those who seek the LORD understand it fully.**

One of the things that happens to you when you become a child of God is the fact that you begin to see things clearly. You have a clearer understanding of life. It's like when the United States Treasury trains someone to detect counterfeit money. They have them handle the real money eight hours a day. When they come across something that is false they are able to recognize it immediately because they have handled and studied the original so intently.

You gain an understanding when you are closely tied to something. When you are an evil, godless person there is no way you can understand justice. It just doesn't make any sense to you. You ask questions like, "How could God do such a thing?" "Why did God allow that to happen?" But when you seek the Lord and know Him and His ways you begin to understand things more fully! The light comes on. God is a loving God but He is also a just God. There are consequences to our actions and God Almighty is the Judge of the universe.

There is coming a day when justice will be served. Praise God that He has made a way for us to be justified...*just as if I'd* never sinned! Thank the Lord that Jesus made a way for us to stand clean before The Judge...our slate completely obliterated by His life's payment! We are in on "the know" now. Let's share the good news with everyone we meet!

"Lord I seek You today. Show me Your heart for those who are lost and dying. Open my eyes to see their hearts. They can't understand until they seek You. Help me to create a thirst in their lives to seek the One and only true God. The One who can make everything clear and bring them life everlasting. I want to know You so well that I have full understanding...I seek You today Lord. Amen."

"Run, run, run!"

Psalm 119:32

**32 I run in the path of your commands,
for you have set my heart free.**

When someone has done something amazing for you, you really don't have a hard time doing something that they ask of you. The Psalmist makes a very simple but profound statement here...I run in the path of Your commands, for You have set my heart free!

I've been married to my wonderful wife Kristie for 30 years now. I'm more in love with her today than when I first married her. She fully has my heart you might say. I would do anything for her...anything she asked of me. In the same way, I've been a Christian now for over 45 years and am more in love with my Savior, Jesus Christ, than I have ever been. I would do anything for Him...anything He asked...and I have! Kristie and I have sold our possessions and started over in ministry 3 times now, at His command. We have walked away from stability and comfort and headed into the unknown at His beckoning. We have never regretted one moment of following His commands. He always has our best interests in mind!

I know exactly what the Psalmist is saying. When your heart has been set free, nothing can keep you from running in the path of the commands of the One who has opened your prison door! It's not like they're commands at all because His commands bring life abundant! You've been set free by Him and your heart is fully His! It doesn't matter what He's asking of you. There's no questioning...no hesitation...no fear...just simply running toward His voice! What is He asking of you today? Run, run, run my friend!

"Lord I choose to run in the path of Your commands today because You have set my heart free! Your commands bring life and why wouldn't I want that? I love You with all my heart and I will follow hard after You because you have my best interests in mind. You have given me life to the fullest. Thank You so much! I'm running toward Your voice today. Give me the courage to say yes to You. I love You Lord. Amen."

"Who you listenin' to?"

Proverbs 28:23

[23] He who rebukes a man will in the end gain more favor than he who has a flattering tongue.

It was one of those tough conversations. I'm sure you've had your share of them as well. My brother Doug had pulled me into his college dorm room and confronted and challenged me on some things. I didn't want to hear it. My mind was made up! Who did he think he was anyway to talk to me like that? Of course my initial reaction was one of defensiveness and putting up walls. I wasn't going to listen to him no matter what! Several days later, after coming to my senses and realizing that he really had my best interest in mind, I made some huge changes and choices that have affected my life in so many positive ways.

The wise man says that a rebuke will gain you more favor...in the end! It may not look like you've made any progress at all, but you can't look at the moment at hand. You've got to look further into the future. The reality is that if you really care about someone, you can't let them continue going down a path that leads to destruction! There will be those who don't really care about you and will come around and tell you that everything is just fine...you're okay to continue living like that! You can always find someone who will pat you on the back and agree with you even though you are headed for disaster. I had plenty of friends that encouraged me in my current state.

When you're off, you need someone who will tell you the truth! You need someone who will confront and rebuke you in love to get you back on track. And you need to be that kind of friend to someone else. In the end you'll gain favor. There may be strain on the relationship at first, but in the end you will gain more favor because you've spoken the truth in love! Who do you need to talk to today? Or maybe who do you need to listen to?

"Lord, help me to be a wise and bold friend. Help me to always speak the truth in love knowing that I could possibly be the only one who really cares enough to do something. Give me Your wisdom and discernment as I walk through this day. Show me what You see and help me to be bold enough to change or to say something beneficial...even if it causes tension for the moment. I know that in the end I'll gain more favor for You have been my guide. Help me to listen to a loving rebuke as well. I love You Lord! Amen."

"Remember who you are!"

1 John 2:29

[29]If you know that he is righteous, you know that everyone who does what is right has been born of him.

I recall many times when I would be leaving the house my Dad would say, "Greg. Remember who you are!" What a bummer that statement was! It really messed up the fun that I was planning on having. I knew what my Dad was saying. Remember that you carry my name. I have given you a name without reproach. I have passed on a good name to you and you had better not mess that up! He was saying that the Hollis name had a reputation...a good reputation. I had the honor of carrying that name and I shouldn't do anything that would bring a stain of regret on it for the future generations.

I wonder if our Heavenly Father is at all concerned about His name that He has so generously lavished on us as His children. We know that He is righteous and our actions really do show whose child we really are. I want to live in such a way that no one has to question whose family I belong to! I want to be such a shining testament to the world of how the Lord has transformed my life!

There really should be no question which family we are a part of. He is righteous and if we do what is right we know that we've been born of Him! I can't tell you how many times I've had someone approach me and say, "You're a Hollis aren't you?" They could simply tell by how I looked and how I acted! Wouldn't it be wonderful if everyone we came in contact with would quickly recognize that we're a part of the family of God? "You're God's kid aren't you?" They will know who you are by how you live! I think it's high time that we remember who we are!

"Lord I thank You for changing me. I thank You that You have cleansed my heart and given me new life. You've adopted me into Your family. Help me to live like it! I want to do what is right. I want the world to see and know that I'm Your child! Help me to remember who I am today! My life is Yours! Amen."

"I can't stay the same!"

1 John 3:6

[6]No one who lives in him keeps on sinning. No one who continues to sin has either seen him or known him.

How do you keep on sinning once you have been set free? How can you go back to that kind of lifestyle when you have met the Savior of your soul? John has a pretty strong opinion here doesn't he? When you live in Him…so filled with Jesus…you can't keep on sinning! He says that if you continue on your sinful, headstrong way then you really haven't seen or known Him at all. Something dramatic happens when we encounter Jesus. His lovingkindness leads us to repentance and changes us from the inside out. For some, the transformation is immediate. Old habits and addictions just disappear overnight. For others the change is more gradual…it's a process. The problem comes when we don't see any change at all. I guess, in that case, the question we would have to ask ourselves is, "Have I really allowed Jesus to be the Lord of my life? Have I given Jesus the throne of my life?" He not only wants to be our Savior…He must be our Lord! When Jesus is Lord then everything changes. I willingly turn over the reigns of my life to Him and allow Him free access to every nook and cranny of my life. I think what John is saying here is, if nothing has changed for you then you must not have had a true encounter with the Risen Lord.

The reality is that you can't stay the same if Jesus is Lord of your life! You can't continue living your same old lifestyle if Jesus is sitting on the throne of your life. There may be certain areas of your life that you have yet to yield to Him. Why not do that today before you walk away from this moment?

"Dear Lord Jesus I invite You to take full control of me today. I need Your forgiveness for (   ). Please come and totally transform me by Your power. I yield my life to You. When I get off track and start to drift back into my old habit patterns, please convict me and lead me in the way everlasting! I will follow You today and always! Amen."

I am what I am today because of the choices I made yesterday!

"Come on and look up!"

Psalm 121

[1] I lift up my eyes to the hills—
where does my help come from?

[2] My help comes from the LORD,
the Maker of heaven and earth.

[3] He will not let your foot slip—
he who watches over you will not slumber;

[4] indeed, he who watches over Israel
will neither slumber nor sleep.

[5] The LORD watches over you—
the LORD is your shade at your right hand;

[6] the sun will not harm you by day,
nor the moon by night.

[7] The LORD will keep you from all harm—
he will watch over your life;

[8] the LORD will watch over your coming and going
both now and forevermore.

The hills were filled with riches and treasure. The hills were a mighty stronghold in battle. You could see your enemy from afar and be able to attack with strength from the hills. In the natural you would think that the hills would be all the advantage you would need. All the money and military savvy you could possibly want were found there. And yet when all is said and done the Psalmist declares that everything I need is coming from God's hand! My help comes from the Lord! He's the maker of it ALL. His protection, favor and blessing are really all I will ever need. If God is for me then who can be against me? I love the confidence that he has in his God. Do you have that kind of confidence in God today? Is He all you need or do you worry and fret about every little detail of life? We need that same boldness and confidence in God today. He won't let my foot slip! He's not sleeping and unconcerned about the details of my life! The Lord watches over me! His shadow is covering me and providing shade for me to walk every step in! No fear when He is near! He's all about it! I lift up my eyes today and look at the 'hills'. Where does my help come from? I've got to side with the Psalmist today. My help comes from the Lord, the Maker of it all! Come on my friend and look up!

"Lord I turn my eyes to You today. I trust Your promises and know that worldly wealth and provision is only temporary, but You are an Everlasting God! My hope and trust is in You and You alone! I will lift up my eyes and focus on You. You are my God and I thank You for Your constant help and protection that You provide for me even when I don't know You're there. Thank You that Your eyes are always on me. Continue Your amazing work in my life today. I love You Lord! Amen."

"It CAN happen!"

Hosea 5:4

**4 "Their deeds do not permit them
to return to their God.
A spirit of prostitution is in their heart;
they do not acknowledge the LORD.**

Have you ever known someone who loved their habit so much
that it drove them away from the ones they said they loved?
They refused to give up 'their thing' for what truly mattered.
This spirit of prostitution is interesting. They sold themselves
for what truly didn't matter and walked away from Him who
matters most! I've been around long enough to see many
people come to the Lord and then walk away from Him to
follow after gods that can't give life…gods that leave you
devastated. They become so enamored with the things of this
world that their deeds don't permit them to return to God.
They say they want to come back, but they live in such a way
that they can't! They've sold themselves to something that is
destroying them and they can't see a way out. You may have
someone very close to you that is in this same boat. You talk
to them but it seems your words are falling on deaf ears. You
pray for them to come to their senses but see no change.
There is hope! God can replace that spirit of prostitution that is
in their heart and fill them with His Holy Spirit if they will just
acknowledge Him! Maybe there is someone you need to pray
for today. Pray that the Lord will change their heart to simply
acknowledge Him. It can happen! I've witnessed it with my
own eyes. We have dozens of people in our church today who
were written off by everyone as hopeless. They had no hope
as far as the world could see…but God transformed them!
God intervened as a result of someone's continued prayers
and obedience. It could happen for your friend or family
member! Why not bring them before the throne of God today?

"Lord Jesus Christ I bring (   ) to you today and ask You to absolutely set them free from their sins. Release them from the hand of the enemy who has blinded their eyes. Rebuke this spirit of prostitution that is in their heart and let them acknowledge You as Lord and Savior of their life. Just like You did for Paul the apostle, drop the scales from their eyes and let them have a life changing encounter with You! Send someone their way who can reach them where they are. Use me as well. I thank You Lord that You are going to do this in Jesus' Mighty Name! Amen."

"Wow, what a harvest!"

Hosea 10:12

**¹² Sow for yourselves righteousness,
reap the fruit of unfailing love,
and break up your unplowed ground;
for it is time to seek the LORD,
until he comes
and showers righteousness on you.**

I've planted a little bit in my lifetime. I'm not really a farmer but my Mom grew up on a farm and has taught me a few things about farming. When we were younger, we would spend our Christmas vacations on the farm with our grandparents, aunts, uncles and cousins. What a great time we always had. One thing I do know from being around farming a little bit is that the crop doesn't grow overnight. It takes time and much patience to see what you've planted spring up and come to fruition. The preparation of plowing, preparing the ground and planting the seed is almost too much for some people...they're way too impatient. Hosea is declaring that we must break up the hardness of our hearts and plant, plant, plant! If we will do what God asks of us then we will reap an amazing harvest...the fruit of unfailing love. What is he asking us to plant? Righteousness! Right living with God...being right-wise with God and His ways. The fruit of that kind of living will blow your mind. You won't believe the harvest that will be poured out on you in due time! God Himself will come and shower you with His righteousness.

What should you do in the mean time while you're waiting on the fruit? Seek the Lord! Spend time in His presence. Time with God is never wasted time. You may not have an instantaneous answer to your prayers but no time in His presence goes by the wayside as unprofitable. So go ahead. Sow righteousness. Break up the unplowed ground in your life. Plant the seeds that will produce the kind of harvest you really want. Seek the Lord until He comes and downpours on you His righteousness and unfailing love! Wow, what a harvest!

"Lord help me to plant the right kind of seed in my lifetime...seed that will be a blessing to me and to those around me. Help my living to glorify You today. I know that seeds of righteousness will produce amazing fruit...fruit that will remain. I want that kind of fruit in my life. I will wait patiently as I seek You today with all my heart and soul. You are Amazing God! I love You. Amen."

"You don't need to go..."

Amos 5:4-5

**4 This is what the LORD says to the house of Israel:
"Seek me and live;**

**5 do not seek Bethel,
do not go to Gilgal,
do not journey to Beersheba..."**

There have been several times in my lifetime that I've seen people travel thousands of miles to a place where God was moving to receive some kind of impartation. I remember Brownsville Florida, Toronto Canada and most recently Lakeland Florida where a move of God would break out and thousands of people would flock to see what God was doing and to try to receive something special in their lives. It almost became cultish in my estimation. The question was always, "Have you been yet?" Somehow it seemed to become all about the place and not about God.

It was during the Brownsville revival days that I was reading my One-Year Bible and read this passage. It was as if the Lord was saying to me...you don't have to go 'somewhere' to find my presence and power. All you need to do is seek ME and you will live! You don't need to run here and there to find and experience a move of God. You just need to seek the Lord! He has everything you need in His hands. I was privileged to attend the Brownsville Revival several times over those next few years because our family was traveling as evangelists and would sometimes pass that way. I watched people stand in line for hours waiting to get into the church to experience a God moment. I couldn't help but think that if they had that same anticipation and faith back at their home church, then they would probably receive the same kind of powerful moment from God that they got there. You really don't need to travel thousands of miles to meet the Lord and receive something powerful from Him. He is right here, right now, waiting to show Himself strong in your behalf! Seek Him and you will LIVE!

"Lord help me to recognize You right here where I am. I know that You have special things for me...even today. I commit to seeking after You with my whole heart because You are the source of life. You can touch me right here in this moment. I seek Your face today Lord. Amen."

"Anointed to confront"

Micah 3:8

**8 But as for me, I am filled with power,
with the Spirit of the LORD,
and with justice and might,
to declare to Jacob his transgression,
to Israel his sin.**

Don't you hate it when you have to confront someone when they're living wrong? It's probably one of my least favorite things to do in life. I've had times when it has gone really good and times when it has gone really, really bad. Sometimes people just don't want to change or even own up to the fact that they are wrong or need to change at all. Those are tough, tense moments…but necessary. Who knows if you might be the only one that God can use in their life at this moment to speak the truth. What we all need in those times is the anointing of God on our life. You need the power of God…His anointing that will break every yoke of bondage. You need His Spirit filling you with all wisdom and strength giving you words that will bring life. You must be filled with all that God is if you are going to declare to someone their transgression and sin. That is why prayer is so vital in preparation for preaching and in confronting someone with their sin. They really are the same in a lot of ways. You are pointing out by the power and Spirit of the Lord what is wrong in their life and needs to change. When you come to someone with that kind of news, you had better have spent some quality time in the Lord's presence so that His anointing gives you the right words to speak. His anointing and power will give you words that will pierce to the heart of the matter and not just deal with superficial, outward things. Maybe there is someone the Lord has been tapping you on the shoulder to deal with. Let God fill you with His Spirit and power…with His justice and might so that you will be able to confront wisely and with great results.

"Lord I'm asking You to fill me with Your power today. Please give me all that I need to speak to those You bring to my attention...my assignment for today. I know that You care for them and want them to turn around and walk with You. Fill me with Your Spirit, with Your justice and might so that I'll be able to say the words that will bring about Your desired goal. I need Your anointing and Your boldness today. Lead me by Your Holy Spirit I pray in Jesus' Name. Amen."

"Though it linger…wait for it"

Habakkuk 2:2-3
[2] Then the LORD replied:
"Write down the revelation
and make it plain on tablets
so that a herald may run with it.

[3] For the revelation awaits an appointed time;
it speaks of the end
and will not prove false.
Though it linger, wait for it;
it will certainly come and will not delay.

What is it about patience? Why do I want what I want, when I want it…NOW!?! We've grown up in a microwave culture that you can push a few buttons and have what you want immediately. Our computers and internet services are becoming so much faster and capable of giving us immediate information. The world is at our fingertips in an instant. But don't make me have to wait a few seconds! I want it now!!! There are times in my life and I'm sure in yours as well that God just doesn't seem to move at lightning fast speed. He speaks to us ever so quietly and confirms in our spirit that He is going to do something and then we sit and wait…and wait…and…wait.

Most people read this scripture and talk about leadership tactics and strategies for sharing vision, and that is all good. But I see the long, long waiting time that the Lord is talking about here as the crux of the matter. Yes, you need to write down the revelation of what the Lord says to you. You must make it plain so everyone can understand what's coming, but is that really the hard part? I don't think it is. God has spoken to me on various occasions and I've gotten so excited thinking it's going to happen today…or next week…or next month. And then the disappointment sets in as I wait. The reality is that God speaks to us to get us ready for what He's going to do…some time! He rarely shows you the date and exact time and for me that's difficult to handle. I know God's going to come through but do I have the patience to hold on for the answer…for the revelation to be fulfilled? If God has spoken; write it down! It's going to happen! He will come through. Though it linger…wait for it. It may not come in your timing but it will certainly come…in God's perfect timing…His appointed time!

"Lord help me to wait on You. You said that if I wait on You I will renew my strength. Thank You for what You have shown me. I will write it down and make it plain so others can understand and see Your power. I will not give up or grow weary in my waiting because I know that You will bring it to pass no matter how long it takes. It will certainly come. Thank You Lord for speaking to me. I am Yours forever. Amen."

Pray the details…it's a great stress reliever!

"Tough Times"

Habakkuk 2:9-10

**[9] "Woe to him who builds his realm by unjust gain
to set his nest on high,
to escape the clutches of ruin!**

**[10] You have plotted the ruin of many peoples,
shaming your own house and forfeiting your life.**

Have you ever been so desperate that you've done something you knew wasn't quite right? You might have had a fear of going under so you did something you weren't all that proud of. From a pastor's standpoint I read this passage in a little different light. There's a problem in the church world called 'proselytizing'. It's the practice of trying to get someone from another church to join your church. Reaching across boundary lines and coaxing sheep from another fold to come try out your much greener pastures. You rationalize that if your church is growing then you'll be ok no matter how it grows. It doesn't really matter what happens at that other church. I would have to call that 'unjust gain' in a sense.

There are moments of desperation in everyone where we are trying to escape the clutches of ruin. The outlook is not good. It may be a bad financial year…attendance may be down…your reports weren't all that sparkly this year…the business across town is flourishing but yours is floundering. How are we going to make it through this recession? Don't stoop to building your realm, whatever your realm is, by unjust gain! It is just not worth it! It's one of those "Woe" moments in the Bible. The result may be a short term gain but the long term result will be the ruin of many and the shaming of your own house. He even goes so far as to say you are forfeiting your life! Nothing sucks the life out of you like doing the wrong thing. I know these may be desperate times, but God has a plan for you right where you are. His plan is to prosper you when you follow His directions for your life, your business or for your ministry. You don't have to build your realm by unjust gain. God will give you everything you need as you seek after Him.

"Lord thank You for the warning. May I not trust in man's tactics but trust in the One who knows everything! I will not build my realm by unjust gain! I will do the right thing today in Your eyes knowing that I'm not forfeiting my life or shaming my house. I will follow You at all cost! You are my God and You want the best for me! Guide me I pray. I love You! Amen."

"Yes, Today Lord!"

Habakkuk 3:2

**² LORD, I have heard of your fame;
I stand in awe of your deeds, O LORD.
Renew them in our day,
in our time make them known;
in wrath remember mercy.**

I've heard the stories like you have. Stories of the mighty moves of God where His power was made known in amazing ways. I've heard of miracles that are mind boggling. My Grandfather had all kinds of stories of God's miraculous power. He prayed for a man whose eyeballs hung out of their sockets and lay on his cheeks. The man was in much pain and my Grandpa Hollis prayed for him and God sucked those eyes right back into place! Grandpa prayed for a man's cow that was sick and wasn't producing the milk that the family needed for survival. That cow began to give more milk than a cow is supposed to give after God touched it! Lord, I have heard of Your fame! I stand in awe of Your deeds, O LORD. My hearts cry is that You would renew them in our day!

I don't want to just tell the stories of the past! I want to be a part of creating stories for the future generations to hear! I've seen miracles in my day. I've prayed for people to be healed and God has miraculously shown up. Elijah, our oldest son had a growth on his neck a couple of years ago that needed surgery. It was about the size of a racquetball. He was getting ready to be married and the surgery would have left a hefty scar on his throat. We told the doctor that we wanted to pray first before we resorted to surgery and see what God would do. After much prayer it disappeared! Our God is an awesome God! He is still the same today as He was yesterday! I'm in awe of His deeds and I want to see more of them today…in my day! I want the miracles of the book of Acts and the

Gospels to become regular fare in my lifetime. I don't want to just hear about it…I want to experience it for myself!

"Lord my prayer is simply what Habakkuk prayed…Lord, I have heard of Your fame; I stand in awe of Your deeds, O LORD. Renew them in our day! In our time make them known O LORD! I want to see Your power unleashed in my generation! Let Your life flow through me to someone in need today in Jesus' Name! Amen."

God deals in absolutes…not comparisons!

"I will rejoice in the Lord...in spite of this!"

Habakkuk 3:17-19

**[17] Though the fig tree does not bud
and there are no grapes on the vines,
though the olive crop fails
and the fields produce no food,
though there are no sheep in the pen
and no cattle in the stalls,**

**[18] yet I will rejoice in the LORD,
I will be joyful in God my Savior.**

**[19] The Sovereign LORD is my strength;
he makes my feet like the feet of a deer,
he enables me to go on the heights...**

Have you ever been there? It seemed like nothing was going right. You were down so low that you had to look up just to see the bottom! I've been there. I know the feeling. It's an awful place to be. And it seems that when you are in slices of time like that is when the enemy of your soul comes and sits on your shoulder and rubs it in. When everything is heading the wrong direction. When all seems to be lost. When there is no hope on the horizon. That's the time to praise the One who is your Lord and Savior. I've found that praise has an amazing effect on poor circumstances. Praise changes the atmosphere! Praising God in the midst of tremendous suffering and loss gives the devil a black eye and sets you in a high place...a place of blessing! I love what he says here...things are bad...nothing is going my way...there's nothing to put my hope in besides the Lord! And He's enough! The Sovereign Lord is my strength. I love that word 'sovereign'. It means having complete, supreme power and authority. The Sovereign Lord...the One who has complete power and authority is the One who is giving me strength right now! He is giving me all that I need. He is teaching me and equipping me to be able to walk through anything! God is making my feet able to walk in very difficult places! I will rejoice in Him! I will be joyful in God my Savior! This is just a 'slice in time' and I will come through with flying colors! Whatever you may be going through today…praise Him! He is your strength. He is helping you navigate the rocky crags. He is enabling you to go to the next level! Praise and rejoice in Him today!

"Lord I praise You today! Yeah, things may not be the best right now but I won't let that dictate my praise. I rejoice in You today. You are my strength! You are my Savior! I can't put my hope in the things of this world…they always let me down. But You are trustworthy. Thank You for helping me walk through this slice of time and navigate every difficult step. I know that You are taking me to new heights! Thank You Lord! I will follow You! Amen."

"Priority Check!"

Haggai 1:2-11

[2] This is what the LORD Almighty says: "These people say, 'The time has not yet come for the LORD's house to be built.' "

[3] Then the word of the LORD came through the prophet Haggai: [4] "Is it a time for you yourselves to be living in your paneled houses, while this house remains a ruin?"

[5] Now this is what the LORD Almighty says: "Give careful thought to your ways. [6] You have planted much, but have harvested little. You eat, but never have enough. You drink, but never have your fill. You put on clothes, but are not warm. You earn wages, only to put them in a purse with holes in it."

[7] This is what the LORD Almighty says: "Give careful thought to your ways. [8] Go up into the mountains and bring down timber and build the house, so that I may take pleasure in it and be honored," says the LORD. [9] "You expected much, but see, it turned out to be little. What you brought home, I blew away. Why?" declares the LORD Almighty. "Because of my house, which remains a ruin, while each of you is busy with his own house. [10] Therefore, because of you the heavens have withheld their dew and the earth its crops. [11] I called for a drought on the fields and the mountains, on the grain, the new wine, the oil and whatever the ground produces, on men and cattle, and on the labor of your hands."

Have you ever asked yourself what you should be doing differently, as you look around and see all the things not going right in your life? Maybe you've wondered if your priorities were all out of whack as you contemplate the situation you're in. These people thought that God's house really didn't matter. They put God and His house on the back burner as they grappled to fulfill their deepest human desires. All that mattered was their own personal comfort and security. The prophet served them notice that the situation they found themselves in was of their own doing. It was because of their wrong priorities that they found themselves working harder and harder and never having enough…eating and drinking but never being satisfied…putting on more and more clothes but never being warm enough. It seemed that they would work their fingers to the bone and their money would grow wings and just fly away. Sound familiar? I wonder if we get so caught up in things that don't last and aren't eternally important that we lose sight of those things that are of lasting eternal value. I don't want to ever be so busy that I neglect the Lord and His house. God told them that the lack that they were experiencing was because of their skewed priorities. God had had enough. He called for a drought on the fields, grain, vineyards, and crops and on men and cattle. God isn't playing around my friend! It's time we give careful thought to our ways…straighten up our priorities and put God and His Kingdom first and foremost. He will add all that other stuff to our lives when we put Him first! When you take a look at your checkbook, how much have you deposited in the Kingdom of God? Time for a priority check!

"Lord forgive me for the times that I'm so busy with my own agenda and put You on the back burner. I'm sorry Lord for not always putting You and Your Kingdom first. Help me to get my priorities straight today. I choose to honor You today above all else. I am giving careful thought to my ways and will adjust my life to prioritize You! I want to experience all You have for me. Thank You Lord for caring enough to confront me. I love You! Amen."

"Watch your eyes dude!"

Proverbs 30:17

[17] "The eye that mocks a father,
that scorns obedience to a mother,
will be pecked out by the ravens of the valley,
will be eaten by the vultures.

I was a youth pastor for about 12 years of my life and was always amazed at the attitude so many young people had with their parents. I grew up in a home where disobedience, talking back or anything close to that was simply never tolerated! I've watched over the years a slippery and steep slide into the pit of mockery of parents and those in authority that brings about certain destruction. It seems every sitcom on TV is filled with that kind of attitude. You just can't live your life like that and expect to walk away unscathed. Do you really want your eyes pecked out by ravens or eaten by vultures? The wise man may be speaking figuratively here, but what if he isn't? Whatever happened to the idea of respecting those in authority over us? The fact of the matter is that you will be blessed in this life and in the life to come as you honor your father and mother. The Bible even promises you that you will live long on the earth when you do! I'd say that's much more appealing than having your eyes ripped out by some wild and wicked birds! Could this even be pertinent to anyone who is placed over you in authority? I think so. Mocking and disobedience just can't bring about blessings…even if it's your boss or supervisor. We should tell our young people and even ourselves at times, "Watch your eyes dude!" Let's get back to where we put those who are in authority over us where they rightfully belong…in a place of honor!

"Lord You know my human tendency for mocking and disobedience. Help me dear Lord to give honor to whom honor is due. I realize that honoring my father and mother is Your first commandment that brings a promise with it. You promised that I would have long life on the earth if I honored my father and mother. I choose to do that today. Thank You for helping me with those in authority over me. I will follow and put my trust once again in You today Lord. Amen."

"Move that mountain!"

Zechariah 4:1-7

[1] Then the angel who talked with me returned and wakened me, as a man is wakened from his sleep. [2] He asked me, "What do you see?"
I answered, "I see a solid gold lampstand with a bowl at the top and seven lights on it, with seven channels to the lights. [3] Also there are two olive trees by it, one on the right of the bowl and the other on its left."

[4] I asked the angel who talked with me, "What are these, my lord?"

[5] He answered, "Do you not know what these are?"
"No, my lord," I replied.

[6] So he said to me, "This is the word of the LORD to Zerubbabel: 'Not by might nor by power, but by my Spirit,' says the LORD Almighty.

[7] "What are you, O mighty mountain? Before Zerubbabel you will become level ground. Then he will bring out the capstone to shouts of 'God bless it! God bless it!' "

Have you ever faced something way beyond your own abilities to handle? Zerubbabel faced an impossible task. I'm sure you've been there before in your life. In fact you may be standing in front of an immovable mountain right now. The Lord asked the prophet Zechariah what he saw. What stood by him was a lampstand with a bowl at the top that fed oil to the lights. The thing that stands out to me is what is beside the lampstand. Two olive trees! It was the olive trees that produced the olive oil that was needed to feed the lampstand lights with a continuous flow of oil. That is exactly what you and I need! We need to have a continual flow of the oil of the

Holy Spirit in our lives. We don't need just a drop or two…we need a continual flow! It's not in our own ability or our mighty power to take on immovable mountains. We need the power of God…the oil of the Holy Spirit continually filling us to move those mighty mountains! The Spirit of God is always available to fill us to overflowing so that we will have all that we need in every circumstance. Nothing is too big for God to take care of! This mountain will become level ground! This impossible situation can't stand before the One who is Able and willing to decimate it! He will give me all that I need to make this mountain crumble and move. 'Not by might nor by power, but by my Spirit,' says the LORD Almighty! This mountain will be moved!

"Lord, once again I look to You for the powerful infilling of Your Holy Spirit. Thank You for a continual flow of Your Spirit in my life to take on every mountain that stands in my way! Flow through me. Give me all that I need to see this mountain come crumbling down. I know it's not my might or power; not my cleverness or human ability; but it's by Your Spirit. Holy Spirit flow through me! Mountain you must move in Jesus' name! Amen."

"Like a magnet to steel."

Zechariah 8:23

23 This is what the LORD Almighty says: "In those days ten men from all languages and nations will take firm hold of one Jew by the hem of his robe and say, 'Let us go with you, because we have heard that God is with you.' "

When was the last time someone walked up to you and grabbed your shirt and said, 'Let us go with you, because we have heard that God is with you.'? Oh, I've seen people push and pull to get near their favorite athlete, rock star or Hollywood celebrity. It's amazing what people will do just to get a glimpse of or an autograph from another human being. There is coming a day when people will clamor for a chance to get near God. I wonder what it would take for that to happen in our day. I wonder if God wants us to stick out so much from the crowd that people see His presence all over us. What if His power was made known in such a real way through us that everywhere we went we were carriers of this incredibly good news? People would hear of the mighty deeds of the Lord and hunt us down to get some of it! What a great day that would be! Is it possible? I believe that it is. God's reputation precedes Him and we are the delivery agents of His miracles. My desire is that there would be such a mighty move of God that people far and wide would be drawn to God's kids. They would be drawn like magnets to steel. They'd have such a hunger and thirst for the things of God that they would search us out. "We have heard that God is with you! Let us go with you!" My heart longs for that day. I want to be smack dab in the center of what God is doing!

"Lord help me to be filled with Your awesome power. Let this world hear of Your amazing reputation and be filled with wonder and awe. Use me Lord! Let Your kingdom come and Your will be done here on the earth...just like it is in heaven! I long for the day when my friends hear that God Almighty is with me! Show Your power and might in my life Lord. Thank You that You are with me! Amen."

"Worthless shepherds need not apply!"

Zechariah 11:15-17

[15] Then the LORD said to me, "Take again the equipment of a foolish shepherd. [16] For I am going to raise up a shepherd over the land who will not care for the lost, or seek the young, or heal the injured, or feed the healthy, but will eat the meat of the choice sheep, tearing off their hoofs.

[17] "Woe to the worthless shepherd,
who deserts the flock!
May the sword strike his arm and his right eye!
May his arm be completely withered,
his right eye totally blinded!"

I guess there's no question what a foolish shepherd looks like according to this passage. A leader who won't care for the lost. A pastor that just won't go after the youth and children, who are really the church of today. Someone in leadership that refuses to bring healing to those who are injured and close to death. Can you even imagine a pastor who won't feed the flock of God that's been entrusted to him? The foolish shepherd only cares about himself. He is using the sheep for his own benefit…devouring them for all their worth. God's not too happy about that kind of shepherd my friend! If God has placed you in leadership then you have a huge responsibility to take care of that which the Lord has put under you.

I've met a few too many foolish shepherds in my lifetime. It's mind boggling to me how anyone could be called of God and head down this foolish path. Woe to the worthless shepherd! Don't desert the flock that God has placed in your care! Dad, don't go after everything else in the world and watch your family go to Hell! Mom, God has put you in place for such a time as this! Take care of the flock that you have oversight of. They need your caring touch. They must have your healing hand guiding and directing them. Feed them from the Bread of Heaven so they will be able to navigate the pathway ahead of them.

"Lord thank You for placing me in the position You have. I will not shirk my responsibilities that You have given me. My desire is to hear You say, "Well done, good and faithful servant!" Give me the wisdom that I need to lead the flock that You have placed me over. I choose to be a wise shepherd…filled with Your words of life! Use me to bring healing, minister life, guide and direct those in my care. In Jesus' Name, Amen!"

"Who are you worshipping?"

Revelation 19:10

[10]At this I fell at his feet to worship him. But he said to me, "Do not do it! I am a fellow servant with you and with your brothers who hold to the testimony of Jesus. Worship God! For the testimony of Jesus is the spirit of prophecy."

John finds himself in the midst of some amazing moments. He's in the presence of Almighty God and is receiving revelation of what is to come. He's overwhelmed to say the least! In that moment he does the unthinkable...he falls at the feet of the delivery agent and begins to worship him! I've witnessed this on so many different levels in the church world. God uses someone to bring a miracle moment to another person and they are immediately put on a pedestal. I've seen God perform miracles for people and watched as those people begin to 'worship' the one who was simply used by God. We hear a word of prophecy and put the one who was used by God to speak His word on a pedestal. This angel and those who are delivery agents for God will declare, "Worship God!" No one who is a true messenger from God wants credit for what they have delivered. They want all the glory to go to the One who is truly deserving. It's all about Jesus my friend! I've seen people get all puffed up about the prophetic things they have received. If we would only realize that the testimony of Jesus is the spirit of prophecy. It really is all about Him! Let's put Jesus in His rightful place. He is King of kings and Lord of lords!

"Lord Jesus Christ I worship You and You alone! Keep my heart and my motives pure as I live and minister for

You. Help me not to become enamored with those around me who are simply Your servants. Help me to keep my focus on You. Use me to be a delivery agent of Your miracle power to someone in need today…and may all the glory go to You, Lord Jesus! Amen."

If you want to get along with God…stay out of His chair!

"So what's your issue?"

Genesis 4:3-7

[3] In the course of time Cain brought some of the fruits of the soil as an offering to the LORD. [4] But Abel brought fat portions from some of the firstborn of his flock. The LORD looked with favor on Abel and his offering, [5] but on Cain and his offering he did not look with favor. So Cain was very angry, and his face was downcast.

[6] Then the LORD said to Cain, "Why are you angry? Why is your face downcast? [7] If you do what is right, will you not be accepted? But if you do not do what is right, sin is crouching at your door; it desires to have you, but you must master it."

Isn't it true that we tend to get angry at God even when we're the ones not doing the right thing? In fact I know people who deliberately disobey the Lord and then turn around and get so mad at Him for not blessing them. Go figure?!? If we'd just learn to do the right thing in every situation we would save ourselves from a lot of problems and misplaced anger. The truth of the matter is that when we don't do what is right, sin is definitely crouching at our door. And it really does desire to have us. I've heard it said that God deals in absolutes, not comparisons! Right is right and wrong is wrong. You can go around comparing yourself to everyone else and make a case that you're just fine. The reality is that there are some absolutes in this life and no amount of comparison is going to change that.

Sin desires to have you, but YOU must master it! If you don't deal effectively with whatever issue it is that's tripping you up, it will tighten its grip around you and eventually destroy you. We all know what happened in Cain's situation...he caved in to the sin and ended up a murderer. The answer? Do what's right! So, what's your issue? You master that sin with God's help and strength and watch the joy in your life return.

"Thank You Lord for reminding me that if I'll just do what is right that I will be accepted! Thank You for accepting me. Thank You for Your grace and mercy that surrounds me. Help me to share all that You are with someone in need today. Use me to help someone else see the truth and walk in freedom. I love You Lord! Amen."

"Just Do It!"

John 2:5

5His mother said to the servants, "Do whatever he tells you."

Nike coined the phrase, "Just Do it!" I'm pretty sure they got it from the Bible though. Another translation of this verse says, "Whatever He says to you, do it." How simple and yet how profound. I heard Francis Chan speaking the other day and he basically said that it's only in Christianity that we 'memorize' what Jesus said instead of DOING what Jesus said! What if I told my daughter Ali to clean her room and she came back to me 2 hours later and said, "Dad, I memorized what you said! In fact I'm having some of my friends over and we're going to discuss what it would look like to clean my room. I've invited some experts in room cleaning to come and lecture us on what a clean room looks like and what it takes to keep it that way. I know this must really please you." What do you think my response would be? It would probably be, "What? No! Don't talk about it...Just Do It!" Somehow in our Christian world we have digressed to the point of talking about, studying, praying about and preaching on what Jesus said to do and really never get around to doing what He said! How tragic! When the servants did what Jesus told them to do, a miracle took place! I wonder if we don't miss out on the amazing miracle power of Jesus in our lives because we just don't do what He tells us to do. We walk all the way around it, but never get around to doing it. What could happen if we all just simply began to DO everything the Lord has asked us to do? I think it would be a powerful movement that would bring the change that this world is longing for! What is He telling you to do? Just Do It!

"Lord please forgive me for all the times I've not done what You've asked me to do. I'm sorry Lord for missing all those miracle moments in life that come as I obey Your clear command. Help me today to listen and obey! I'm choosing to Just Do whatever You ask me to do. I will follow You! Amen."

"SWEET!"

**[29] Since they hated knowledge
and did not choose to fear the LORD,**

**[30] since they would not accept my advice
and spurned my rebuke,**

**[31] they will eat the fruit of their ways
and be filled with the fruit of their schemes.**

Have you ever taken a bite of a nasty piece of fruit? Yuck! It always amazes me when someone who won't listen to godly advice actually gets upset when they reap the outcome of their foolish ways. The wise man makes a pretty strong statement here. He says that those who won't listen hate knowledge. The Lord has tried and tried to get some peoples attention but to no avail. He rebukes, gives advice, tries to get them to pay attention and they just won't have any of it. The outcome is a very scary one! It's scarier than a wicked ugly mask on Halloween! Solomon says that those who live like that will eat the fruit of their ways and be filled with the fruit of their schemes. When all is said and done, they will be eating and living in the outcome of their foolish ways. Yuck again! I'm not the most brilliant person in the world, but that doesn't sound too intelligent to me! When we love knowledge and follow the ways of the Lord there is an amazing blessing that produces fabulous fruit in our lives. I don't know if you've ever bitten into a rotten piece of fruit but it's a shocker to say the least! You prepare your mouth to chomp down on something that looks amazing and end up wanting to spit out what you've bitten off. That's kind of the idea here. Be intelligent enough to love knowledge, fear the Lord, listen to His advice and when He rebukes you, turn around and walk in His ways! If you do, the fruit you'll eat of will be SWEET!

"Tune my ear in to hear Your voice Lord. Help me to shut out every other voice that competes with Yours. I choose to follow Your ways and listen to Your advice. I know You want the best for me. I'm excited about the fabulous fruit that is growing in my life as I fear You Lord! May I have fruit in my life that will be a blessing to someone else today...sweet to the taste. Thank You Lord...I will follow You! Amen."

"It's God calling!"

Isaiah 55:3

**³ Give ear and come to me;
listen, that you may live.
I will make an everlasting covenant with you,
my faithful love promised to David.**

If you have children then you understand what it is for your kids to listen and obey you. One thing that really bothers me is a child that ignores their parents…or anyone in authority for that matter. They hear your voice but choose not to listen. They know you're talking to them but act like they can't hear you! My blood is boiling just thinking about it! It is so dangerous to live like that. I taught my children to listen and obey me at a very young age. Listening and obeying saved their lives! Imagine with me that my child is walking through the grocery store parking lot with me and decides to just run on ahead. From my vantage point I can see that there are cars heading his way. I speak his name and tell him to stop and wait. If he listens and obeys, he will be safe. If he decides to do his own thing, his life could be quickly over! The reason I disciplined my children for not listening was that ignoring their father was hazardous to their health! Your Heavenly Father has a much greater vantage point than you do. He sees all and knows every detail of what is coming your way. He wants the best for you! He wants you to experience life to the fullest extent possible! He wants to fulfill His promises to you, but you hold the key. If you will give ear, listen and come to Him you will find the most amazing life you've ever dreamed of! He's calling…won't you come near Him and listen?

"I'm stopping right now Lord to listen to Your still small voice. Speak to me. Open my ears to hear what Your Spirit would say. I know that You want the best for me. I know that Your plans are amazing and I don't want to miss out on anything that You have for me. Teach me Your ways and I will walk in Your paths. I love You Lord. Amen."

"Firstfruits"

Proverbs 3:9-10

**⁹ Honor the LORD with your wealth,
with the firstfruits of all your crops;
¹⁰ then your barns will be filled to overflowing,
and your vats will brim over with new wine.**

What is it about money that gets everyone so riled up? You start talking about giving to the Lord and suddenly you've hit a brick wall with so many people! "Don't tell me what to do with my money!" they'll say. The wisest man who ever lived on the face of the earth was also one of the richest individuals in history. His wealth would have made Bill Gates look poor! Solomon knew a few things about money and gives us some words of advice. We'd be wise to heed his counsel. Honor the Lord with your wealth! Put God first in your finances so He can bless the rest! Notice he says to honor the Lord with the firstfruits. The firstfruits were simply that…the first fruits that were gathered together. The first check I write after receiving my paycheck is the tithe that belongs to God. I want the first thing that goes out of my storehouse to be God's Tenth. He is the One who has given me the ability to gain wealth and so I honor Him with the first fruits that come my way. Solomon goes on to say that if you'll do that…God's hand of blessing will be upon everything else! Don't wait to see if you have enough to go around, to pay your bills…Honor God first! In this agricultural setting, Solomon is talking about having more crops than your barns can handle, if you'll honor God first. In today's language, God will bless your bank account with an overflow…so much that you'll have to give some away! That's what I'm talking about! Bring it on Lord!

"Lord, I don't want to be foolish with the money You've blessed me with. I want to follow Your plan for my finances. I choose to Honor You today with my wealth...the wealth You've allowed me to have. I will give You the firstfruits of ALL my earnings. I know that You will bless me with an overflow as I honor You! I put You first today Lord Jesus Christ! Thank You for the abundant blessings that You are pouring out in my life! I honor You today! Amen."

"What's your gift?"

Proverbs 18:16

**[16] A gift opens the way
and ushers the giver into the presence of the great.**

I remember moments in my life standing in front of crowds of great people and singing. I think in the back of my mind I was thinking, "How'd I get here?" God gives each of us gifts that, if we choose to nurture those gifts, will bring us into the presence of the great! Growing up I always used to enjoy singing. I would sit for hours by the record player (remember those?) and spin some of my favorite discs, trying to mimic the runs and intonation that the artists had so diligently crafted. I began to grow the gift that God had given me. I ended up entering talent competitions and even winning! Over the years I've been privileged to use the gift that God has blessed me with in many different arenas. I've sung to massive crowds filled with great people. I've also sung to small crowds and been blessed just the same. I believe everyone has a special gift given by God. It's up to us to build on what God has blessed us with. For some it may be the ability to craft words and speak. For others it is a gift of fixing things that break. Still others are on the creative end of things. They design and build and find themselves overseeing projects from the ground up. I don't know what your gift is, but I do know that if you'll nurture that gift that God has blessed you with, you'll find yourself in some pretty amazing places! God wants to use your gift to usher you into the presence of the great. So what's your gift? Open it up and let it open the way for you.

"Lord thank You for giving me the ability to (   ). I realize that this is a gift from You. Help me to recognize how You've blessed me and help me to expand and grow this gift so that I will be able to minister more powerfully than I've ever dreamed of. Use me, as I walk through the doors of opportunity, to be Your messenger of life and hope. I will honor You with the gifts You have given me. I love You Lord. Amen."

The difference between what you ARE and what you WANT to be is what you DO!

"What are you really made of?"

Matthew 11:19b

[19] ...But wisdom is proved right by her deeds."

Some people can really talk a good talk. To hear them speak you would think that they have it all together. The problem is that when you hang around them for a long period of time, you find that their actions don't match their words. I've had the privilege of meeting some famous folk who from a distance seem to have it totally together. You hear them on television and see them from a bystanders view and you'd think they were the real deal. The closer you get though; you begin to see some deep flaws. I've been disappointed more times than I care to think about. Jesus said that wisdom is proved right by her deeds. You find out how wise a person really is by what they actually do! It's not what you say that is the proof of your wisdom...it's what you do that counts. You can talk, talk, talk and slather on at the mouth all you want, but show me your wisdom! Prove it! I wonder if that's why this Christian life is best lived in community? Isn't that what family is all about too? When we are rubbing shoulders every day with one another we are able to really see what we are made of. Anyone can live the Christian life in isolation. It's when you have to actually deal with other people that you find out what kind of wisdom you really have! I wonder what kind of deeds the Lord is asking you to do to prove the wisdom you say you have. Anything come to mind? Go for it my friend! Show what you're made of!

"Lord, I don't want to be just a talker...I want to be a doer! Help my life to be a reflection of You and the wisdom You have placed in me. When people get close to me, may they find me genuine and full of wisdom from above! I really do need You Lord! Guide me today as I walk through this life. I once again ask for Your wisdom today in Jesus' Name! Amen."

"Here is someone special!"

Genesis 41:38

³⁸ So Pharaoh asked them, "Can we find anyone like this man, one in whom is the spirit of God?"

Pharaoh's question was about Joseph. Oh, we know the story of Joseph don't we? Talk about unfair! We love the end of the story but can't believe what it took to get there. Jealousy, betrayal, hatred, lies, false accusations, being forsaken and forgotten even when he was doing everything right! How do you behave when things don't go the way you thought they should? I mean, really! God gave Joseph a sneak peek into his future, and none of what happened to him over the course of those many years seemed to even come close to resembling *anything* God said!

What would you have done? Would you be like so many who cash in their faith in God when things don't go the way they thought they were going to go? Not Joseph. Nothing could shake his faith. No string of seemingly bad luck could deter him from the path that God had him on. He set his face like a flint. He didn't waver. He knew what God had promised and he wasn't giving up until he saw it come to fulfillment. Everywhere he found himself, he worked so hard that he was promoted to the top…even in prison! When he finally stepped into Pharaoh's presence and shared his God-given ideas, it became obvious to all who were there…Here is someone special! Here is the leader we've been looking for! Here is the leader that can take us to the next level. The spirit of God is in this man! That's what I want said about me…the spirit of God is in this man and has set him apart for such a time as this!

"Lord, no matter how bad the circumstances get in my life, help me to follow You all the way. I know You have amazing plans for me. Let me be the kind of person who has Your Spirit so obviously inside of me that it spills out. May those around me notice Your Spirit in me as I live my life today. Help me to live in such a way that brings honor and glory to Your name. Fill me to overflowing with Your Holy Spirit I pray in Jesus' name. Amen."

Character is what a person is in the dark!

"Get your thoughts right!"

Psalm 19:14

[14] **May the words of my mouth and the meditation of my heart
be pleasing in your sight,
O LORD, my Rock and my Redeemer.**

I read the other day where Myles Munroe said that thoughts are silent words. Everything in life starts in the form of a thought. Therefore, a word is an exposed thought! The Psalmist had it right didn't he? The meditation of our heart is where the words of our mouth form. Wouldn't it make a whole lot of sense to get God's thoughts in our heads and in our hearts? How much better off we would be in life if we would get control of our thought life by putting God's Word deep in our hearts. The heart is the fertile seedbed of our words and life isn't it? What you meditate on you eventually become. The wise man also said that as a man thinks in his heart...so IS he! What you dwell on-you become. If the words (those exposed thoughts...those things that I have consistently meditated on) of my mouth and the meditation of my heart is pleasing in the Lords' sight...life is gonna be sweet! When my words and thoughts please my Lord, then I won't have to worry what anyone else thinks!

"O Lord I ask You today to help me meditate on the right stuff. Help me to keep my mind dwelling on good things today...things that are upright and pure...Thoughts that will bring about a fabulous, life giving harvest in my life. I choose to think on good things today. I need Your help Lord to navigate away from every evil, vindictive, unfruitful, impure and wrong thought. I want my thoughts and words to be pleasing to You Lord. Thank You Lord for redeeming my thought life in Jesus' Name. Amen!"

"When God flexes!"

Psalm 21:13

**[13] Be exalted, O LORD, in your strength;
we will sing and praise your might.**

How strong is your God? Is he bigger and stronger than The Hulk? Oh Yeah! When I was a teenager going to Youth Camp there was a body builder who would work out in the bathroom at night. He had a magical device called "The Bullworker" that he used to shape and tone his muscles. We would stand around and marvel at the massive muscles Del had. We were all scrawny little teenagers and here was a soon to be man who had far surpassed anything we had ever seen in our day with his body. We were in awe. I wonder what would happen if we could see the Lord as He really is? In my heart of hearts I truly believe that we would be blown away. We would stand in amazement at His strength and ability! As we see God's hand at work in our lives and begin to exalt Him for who He really is we will be in awe of Him. Be exalted, O Lord, in Your strength, the psalmist prayed, and we will sing and praise Your might! There are times I pray that God would flex his muscles and show who the real boss is! When He does…miracles happen and I shout to the mountain tops of His might. It brings me back to camp days when the word went around that Del was working out in the bathroom! "Hurry everyone, come see him flex his muscles!" Oh that we would proclaim His praise just like that…"Hey everyone…God is flexing His muscles…come and see!"

"Lord I pray today that You would open my eyes to see You as You really are. Help me to see the many times that You have shown Yourself strong and maybe I've been too busy or too blind or distracted to see You and I've missed

it. May You be exalted today O Lord in Your strength. Thank You for flexing Your muscles. Thank You for showing Yourself strong on my behalf. I WILL sing and praise Your might! I WILL declare Your greatness! You O Lord are mighty and I praise You today! There is none like You in all the earth! Amen!"

"Worship ignited!"

Exodus 4:31

[31]...**And when they heard that the LORD was concerned about them and had seen their misery, they bowed down and worshiped.**

Have you ever had a time in your life when things were really miserable? Life just stunk real bad! If you had a friend that sensed what was going on and just showed some concern it made all the difference in the world. They didn't have to have all the answers. They didn't need to hold your hand all day long. They were just genuinely concerned, did what they could and that was enough! Sometimes it just helps to know that God knows what's going on and is concerned. God had called Moses to be the deliverer for His people who were slaves in Egypt. Moses finally said yes to God and headed back to Egypt to meet with the people of God. When he told them all that the Lord had said and that he was there to lead them out they were overjoyed! They finally knew that the Lord had seen their misery and was so concerned about them that He sent someone to help them out of their mess. The result was true worship from the heart! They bowed down and worshiped!

I wonder if we could just simply realize the extent that God has gone to for us. Talk about concern! He loved us so much that He gave His one and only Son as a sacrifice for our sin. He is so concerned that He came to rescue us from eternal death and freely give us eternal life! He is unlocking our prison doors and setting us free if we'll simply let Him! Shouldn't that ignite the biggest firestorm of worship we've ever seen?

"Lord I am amazed at how You love me! What an extent You went to on my behalf! I'm blown away by Your concern for me...little ole me. I worship You with all my heart and soul! I praise Your holy name with everything in me! You are awesome Lord! May this worship that I have in my heart never die out. Awesome Almighty God I praise You today! I bless You Lord with all that I am! Amen!"

"Keep your hands clean!"

Psalm 26:6-7

**⁶ I wash my hands in innocence,
and go about your altar, O LORD,
⁷ proclaiming aloud your praise
and telling of all your wonderful deeds.**

I hate dirty hands! That's probably one of the reasons I wouldn't make a good mechanic…not the only reason mind you, but definitely one of the many reasons ☺. Dirty hands get everything they touch dirty. I hate it when I take my car in to get it fixed and when I get it back the steering wheel is filthy with grease! Dirty hands leave smudge marks on everything they touch. You need a powerful cleanser to take care of grease like that. There's another sure way to stay clean. Don't touch anything that's dirty! Stay innocent! Oh you still need to wash your hands but as you do, you are simply getting rid of the daily grime. When we keep our lives innocent in God's presence, it's a joy to go near His altar! There's no hesitancy or trepidation. When we distance ourselves from that which contaminates body and spirit we are free to proclaim God's praise. We are unencumbered by the things of this world and can loudly declare the wonderful works of the Lord in our lives! I'm so glad, just like you probably are that the Bible says we can come boldly into His presence and find grace and mercy in our time of need. He wants us to keep our hands clean, but He also wants us to come to Him when we are filthy! He's the only One who can make us completely clean! Come before Him today and wash your hands. You deserve it and you'll be glad you did! It will affect everything you touch. You might even give out a shout of praise for all He's done!

"Lord I come before You today to wash my hands and my heart. Please cleanse me and keep me clean in Your sight. I want to please You in all I say and do. I thank You that I am Your child. You love me beyond measure. You and You alone can make me clean! I will proclaim Your praise aloud! I will declare Your wonderful deeds! With my mouth I will bless You and with my hands I will honor You! You are my God and I will follow You wholeheartedly! Thank You for Your cleansing power! Amen."

"No empty hands here!"

Exodus 23:15

15 "Celebrate the Feast of Unleavened Bread; for seven days eat bread made without yeast, as I commanded you. Do this at the appointed time in the month of Abib, for in that month you came out of Egypt. "No one is to appear before me empty-handed.

How much has God done for you? I mean, if we could actually calculate the cost wouldn't it be astronomical? And if we could figure out the savings of what He has kept us from...the benefits of doing things His way...the medical bills we haven't had to pay because He has kept us healthy. How about the blessing of walking in wisdom and not having to pay stupid consequences for bad behavior? The untold times that He has guided us around or through a mess and brought us to our desired haven. The accidents we've avoided because His hand was upon us. Seriously...how much has God done for you? Mistakes you didn't make because you listened to His still small voice. Money you didn't throw at something because He delivered you from a bad habit or addiction. Fights you didn't get into because He helped you control your temper and words. Really...how much has God done for you? Add it up. Try to calculate the savings. If you're anything like me it would range into the millions of dollars! And that's just the money side of things! Is it really too much to ask that you not appear before Him empty-handed? I think not! I am sick and tired of stingy Christians. All He asks is for a portion; a tenth; the firstfruits of all that He's blessed us with. Are we really that selfish that we come into His presence empty-handed? Seriously...How much has God done for you? He deserves our best! No empty hands here!

"Dear Lord I pray that you would make me generous! I don't ever want to be categorized as stingy in Your sight. Thank You for all that You have done for me. I'm overwhelmed at the price that You've paid for my salvation. I'm humbled to think that You have given and given so much for me. Thank You for setting me free! Thank You for all that You are keeping me from! I am forever indebted to You. Let Your spirit of generosity flow in and through me in Jesus' Name. Amen."

"The Promise is connected to a Premise!"

Exodus 23:20-26

[20] "See, I am sending an angel ahead of you to guard you along the way and to bring you to the place I have prepared. [21] Pay attention to him and listen to what he says. Do not rebel against him; he will not forgive your rebellion, since my Name is in him. [22] If you listen carefully to what he says and do all that I say, I will be an enemy to your enemies and will oppose those who oppose you. [23] My angel will go ahead of you and bring you into the land of the Amorites, Hittites, Perizzites, Canaanites, Hivites and Jebusites, and I will wipe them out. [24] Do not bow down before their gods or worship them or follow their practices. You must demolish them and break their sacred stones to pieces. [25] Worship the LORD your God, and his blessing will be on your food and water. I will take away sickness from among you, [26] and none will miscarry or be barren in your land. I will give you a full life span.

I love the promises of God…and I'll wager that you do too! My heart thrills when I read that God wants to bless me and lead me to places, people and things that will be for my ultimate good. I am so excited to know that He is sending angels ahead of me to guard me and to bring me to what He has prepared. Talk about an armed guard escort! God is amazing! I guess what throws a wrench into the promises is the fact that if I want what He has promised then I must do my part and obey what He asks of me! Oh, we don't like to be told what to do, do we? We want to be our own boss! We have rights you know! Nobody is going to tell us what to do!

God will fight for you if you'll simply submit your life completely to Him and follow His ways! He will go ahead of you and deal with things so you don't have to. He will make a place for you and bring you there safely. He will wipe out your enemies…you won't even have to fight! He will bless you abundantly in all that you do! The promise comes with a premise…Don't rebel…Listen carefully…Do what He says…Worship the Lord your God only…and He will do what He promised! God always keeps His end of the bargain! His desire is to bless you and pour out His favor on you. All He wants is your whole-hearted devotion! Sounds like a bargain to me!

"Lord I thank You for Your promises today. Your promises are yes and amen! You say "yes" and I simply agree! I agree with You today and I give my life once again wholeheartedly to You…holding nothing back! Thank You for going ahead of me and making a way for me. Thank You for taking care of things that I don't even know You're taking care of. I will show up today and follow You with everything in me. I will not rebel but I will listen and obey You. Amen."

"Clothes make a man?"

Exodus 28:2

² Make sacred garments for your brother Aaron, to give him dignity and honor.

I'm a 'jeans and t-shirt' kind of a guy. I've never been real concerned about image I guess. Comfort is way more important to me than the 'look'. If you ever see me lookin' fine then you'll know that Kristie, my amazing wife of 30 years definitely had something to do with it! She started dressing me before we were even married! I've always heard that clothes make a man but I'm not sure I agree totally with that. I've met some people who dress up real nice on the outside, but inside they are a complete mess. My Father in Law, Dave Kyllonen, says that you should not dress for the job you are in, but that you should dress for the job you want! I get what he's saying…but I've always had the job I wanted so I've always dressed the way I wanted ☺. When God says to make sacred garments for dignity and honor though, it makes a lot of sense to me. God wanted Aaron and the priests to stand out from the crowd so that everyone who saw what they were wearing would recognize them and set them apart as wholly dedicated to the Lord. They were special people set apart for the Lord's service and God wanted them to have dignity and to be honored among the people.

I wonder what the Lord wants for us today. Do you think He really cares so much about what you wear on the outside or more about what's happening on the inside of your life? When you get to the New Testament you find Jesus telling the teachers of the Law and the Pharisees that they looked good on the outside. He said they had the right clothes on…everyone recognized them by their outfits…but they were full of dead men's bones! You can dress up a pig, but when you take the clothes off all you've got is a whole lot of pork!

What's going on *inside* of you today? Is Jesus really the Lord of your life inside? Do you have dignity and honor where it really matters most? Oh go ahead and dress for success, but make sure you've got true success on the inside!

"Lord Jesus Christ I need You to dress me in sacred garments on the inside of my life. I guess I really do care what everyone thinks of me on the outside but I care more about what You see on the inside of me! Clean me out oh Lord! Dress me for true success in this life and in the life to come...inside and out! I give my heart and life fully and completely to You

"Safe in His Hands!"

Psalm 31:14-15a

**[14] But I trust in you, O LORD;
I say, "You are my God."
[15] My times are in your hands;**

Trust. It's a small word with a huge assignment. What do I really trust in? Right now I'm trusting in my chair to hold me up and not let me down! Oh, I've put my trust in a lot of chairs that have let me down in the past but somehow I just keep trusting in chairs…kind of crazy isn't it. I wonder why we put our trust in things that have disappointed us in the past and won't put our trust in God. For me, I would have to say that the only one who hasn't disappointed me in my life has been God! He has had my back…and my front my entire life! When you put your full trust in the Lord you can confidently say with the Psalmist David, "You are my God." My times are in Your hands!" David had seen his share of trouble and heartache. He had been through quite a lot of disappointment from those he should have been able to trust…family, close friends and confidants. Sound familiar? We all have faced great trials and disappointments and for some of us it drives us to distrust anyone…ever again! We vow that we will never be hurt by anyone else again. We close ourselves off from anyone and everyone…including God. Just because you've been hurt over and over again doesn't mean there is no one left to trust. You can throw caution to the wind like David did and say, "But I trust in YOU, O LORD!"   I remind you that the Lord has your best interest in mind! He has amazing plans for you! He wants you to prosper and be blessed! He really is trustworthy! If God is for you, and you know deep down inside that He is, then you can confidently place yourself and your times in His hands! In His hands is a very safe place to be and His timing is impeccable. Just ask David!

"Lord, I choose to find safety in Your hands today! I put my whole trust and faith in You and You alone. You will not fail me or forsake me. You are an amazing God! I confidently place my times in Your hands. I will not fret when I don't see what I think I need to see. I can't see everything, but You can and You are working ALL things together for my good! I trust in You Lord...You are my God...my times are in Your hands! Thank You for taking care of me! I love You Lord. Amen."

You can't harvest a crop before you plant it!

"How willing are you?"

Exodus 35:21-29

[21] and everyone who was willing and whose heart moved him came and brought an offering to the LORD for the work on the Tent of Meeting, for all its service, and for the sacred garments. [22] All who were willing, men and women alike, came and brought gold jewelry of all kinds: brooches, earrings, rings and ornaments. They all presented their gold as a wave offering to the LORD. [23] Everyone who had blue, purple or scarlet yarn or fine linen, or goat hair, ram skins dyed red or hides of sea cows brought them. [24] Those presenting an offering of silver or bronze brought it as an offering to the LORD, and everyone who had acacia wood for any part of the work brought it. [25] Every skilled woman spun with her hands and brought what she had spun—blue, purple or scarlet yarn or fine linen. [26] And all the women who were willing and had the skill spun the goat hair. [27] The leaders brought onyx stones and other gems to be mounted on the ephod and breastpiece. [28] They also brought spices and olive oil for the light and for the anointing oil and for the fragrant incense. [29] All the Israelite men and women who were willing brought to the LORD freewill offerings for all the work the LORD through Moses had commanded them to do.

Here we go talking about money again! I know, right? Every time you turn around the Bible is talking about money and giving! Could it be that the stuff we have and want to keep for ourselves is part of our problem? Jesus talked more about money than He did about heaven and hell combined! He really did think it was a big deal. I find it interesting that this passage has the word "willing" in it four times.

Verse 29 says that the Israelites were commanded by the Lord through Moses to bring a 'freewill' offering for the work of building the Tabernacle. But not everyone did! Only those who were 'willing' brought their stuff to God for His work! I wonder what everyone else did?

That was them…but what about us? Every time the offering bucket is passed in church what do you do? Are you willing or are you holding on stingily to what the Lord has blessed you with? Are we willing to let go of what's in our hands so God can let go of what's in His hand? I'm convinced that we somehow squelch the blessings of God that He wants to pour out on us by our greed and selfishness. When we gave our kids a candy bar when they were young, we would always ask for a bite of it at some point. What were we doing? We were cultivating a giving spirit in our children. When they refused to give us a bite we would take the whole thing away! Sounds cruel doesn't it? It worked! They eventually became 'willing' to give back what we had blessed them with! How willing are you today? What is God asking you to bring to Him? Is it worth hanging on to? I think not! Go ahead…be willing…someday you'll be glad you were!

"Lord please give me a willing spirit today. I want to be willing to do anything You ask of me. I am willing to give You anything You want from me…including my money. I know that 'selfish' is how I came into this world but I want to leave this world different! Help me to be a generous giver! Make my heart a willing heart…able to hear Your still small voice and obey every detail. I love You Lord and I am willing to follow You in everything! Amen."

"Ignorance is no excuse!"

Leviticus 4:13

13 "'If the whole Israelite community sins unintentionally and does what is forbidden in any of the LORD's commands, even though the community is unaware of the matter, they are guilty.

We've all heard the stories. Someone breaks the law and pleads ignorance. The judge thinks for one second and then declares, "Ignorance of the law excuses no man!" I know I've done it! "But officer, I didn't know what the speed limit was!" No excuse! I was wrong and I paid the fine. Ok, that's all fine and good, but how am I supposed to know all of God's laws and commands? The truth is that He has written them on our hearts. You really do know when you're doing something wrong! When you've given your life to Jesus Christ, His Holy Spirit is in you to guide and direct you every moment of your life. He shows you truth and leads you in the way you should go. You aren't ignorant…you can't be!

He wants you to succeed and so He will gently nudge you the right way. Oh you can push Him away and ignore His still small voice, but that truly would be ignorant! I don't want to live ignorantly and neither do you. The great thing about all of this is that Jesus Christ offers complete and total forgiveness! He will remove our transgressions from us as far as the east is from the west! All we have to do is humble ourselves and ask for His grace and mercy. He is faithful even when we are unfaithful.

Its funny how we can get upset at the police officer when he pulls us over for an infraction when all the time it is our breaking of the law that has brought it on. I remember my Dad driving me somewhere and I saw a cop on the side of the road. I yelled out, "Dad, there's a cop! Watch out!" He proceeded to tell me that when I'm obeying the law that policemen are simply there for my freedom and protection! Wouldn't it be a much better life to simply obey the laws of the land and live in freedom? That's what God wants for us! We can do it and He will help us!

"Lord I ask You to forgive me today of all the sin I have willfully and/or unintentionally committed. Cleanse my life Oh Lord of all that is against You. Help me to tune my ear into Your voice and obey Your every command. I know that Your commands are for my good and so I will follow You with full abandon! Thank You for Your love and mercy that follow me all the days of my life. I love You Lord. Amen."

"Overwhelming!"

Leviticus 9:6

6 Then Moses said, "This is what the LORD has commanded you to do, so that the glory of the LORD may appear to you."

There were so many things to do and laws to follow for the Israelites. I'm guessing that it was a bit overwhelming at times. I wonder how I would have handled all of that if I lived back then. I want to think that I would have done everything that God asked of me so I could see the glory of the Lord, but I'm not sure. I think I would have gone to any length to hang out with God and see His glory but I guess I'll never know. I'm so glad I don't have to live in the 'what if's' of life, I get to live right in the here and now today. And one thing I'm very thankful for today is the fact that the veil has been torn from the top to the bottom! God did it! He ripped the holy veil! He made access to the Holy of Holies for you and me!

The way into God's presence has been opened by Him and you and I can freely and boldly come into His presence any time, day or night! Jesus Christ became that complete sacrifice that makes a way for us to experience the glory of the Lord and to have a relationship with the God of the universe! How amazing is that? How marvelous...how wonderful! Have you thanked the Lord for the sacrifice He made for you yet today? Have you paused to reflect on the reality that God wants to be with you and has torn down every barrier for that to happen? Have you thanked Him for His love and mercy? Overwhelming isn't it? That the God of the universe wants to fellowship and hang out with me...unfathomable! My part is complete surrender. He's done everything else!

"Lord I'm in awe of Your great love for me today. I'm overwhelmed that You love me so much. Thank You for Your great sacrifice that gives me life and total access to You! Thank You for caring so much for me that You gave of Yourself so freely. Lord I'm amazed at how You love me. I give myself to You in total and complete surrender once again today. Take my life and let it be completely consecrated Lord to Thee! I love You. Amen."

"Crabby Christians!"

Psalm 45:7

[7] You love righteousness and hate wickedness; therefore God, your God, has set you above your companions by anointing you with the oil of joy.

Have you ever met a Crabby Christian? It's an oxymoron isn't it? I think Christians become crabby when they want to live with one foot in the world and one foot in the kingdom of God. Now that's miserable living! I remember living that way for awhile as a teenager. I really did have a great life. I had godly parents that loved me and set a wonderful example of Christ likeness for me to follow. I was raised in an amazing church where we had some truly wonderful people who lead us. The problem was that I wasn't so sure that the faith of my fathers was going to be MY faith! I decided that I was going to be my own man and do things my way! I wanted to serve God but I also wanted to spread my wings and dabble in the worldly. That was an awful time in my life! I've met a lot of 'seasoned' Christians who seem to be doing the same thing. They want to serve God, but only on their terms. Part of them wants to go after God and His ways and the other part longs for the things of this world. That's a miserable way to live! I know from firsthand experience! The Psalmist says that when you love righteousness…God's way of doing things, and hate wickedness then God sets you above everyone else. You will stand out from the crowd. God anoints your life with the oil of JOY! Yeah, that's right; Joy is yours when you go all out for God! Joy covers you when you love righteousness and hate wickedness. There's no better life than a life filled with Joy. The duplicitous life is a wretched life! It's full of misery and regret. Become single minded…go all out for God today and let Him cover you with His Joy! Trust me; you'll be glad you did!

"Lord I don't want to be a crabby Christian. I don't want my life to be divided. I want to love You and serve You with all that I am. I do love righteousness and hate wickedness. I thank You that You will set me in a higher place than I've ever been and anoint my life with the oil of joy! I need Your joy! I need You! Thank You for an undivided heart. You are my God and I love You today with everything in me! Amen!"

"Blessing with no trouble!"

Proverbs 10:22

22 The blessing of the LORD brings wealth, and he adds no trouble to it.

Ok, I admit it. I've entered the Publisher's Clearing House sweepstakes. There, I said it! I know, I know…I feel a little stupid every time I waste the price of a postage stamp and the time it takes to find all the 'special stickers' in their packet, but there's always that slim chance that I'll be the one they surprise with the big check someday! Right?!?! Call me crazy if you want, but who knows…it might just be me! Really, it might! I don't really have aspirations of being wealthy; it would just be nice to not have to worry about having enough money to pay the bills and do some of the extra things we've always dreamed of doing. I have to admit I've met a few wealthy people in my lifetime and I'd have to say for the most part they aren't all that happy. Go figure. That's when I take a step back and look at my life and my family and the ministry that God has so blessed me with and I ponder what true wealth really is. Is it wrapped up in money and things? I think not. I don't know anyone on their death bed who is longing to make another buck to leave to someone else. When you live God's way and have His blessing on your life it brings about a wealth that this world can't give. In fact the blessing of the Lord brings wealth, and He adds no trouble to it! Imagine that…no trouble! Blessing with no trouble! Wealth with no trouble added! What an amazing God! He really does want the best for us. He wants to bless us with unfathomable blessings. Go ahead…take an inventory of your wealth. You'll find that what the Lord brings your way is truly blessed! Oh, I'll probably keep entering the sweepstakes…just in case…but my heart is steadfastly set on the Lord!

"Thank You Lord for Your blessing that You bring my way. I truly am blessed indeed! I am wealthy in ways this world can never know. You have blessed me abundantly and I am forever grateful. Please help me keep my eyes focused on You and on eternal things. Guide and direct me when I want to stray from Your hand of blessing. I long for You and the true wealth that You bring. Thank You for the reminder! I love You Lord. Amen."

"Shhhhhh…He is God!"

Psalm 46:10

[10] "Be still, and know that I am God;
I will be exalted among the nations,
I will be exalted in the earth."

I'm a musician and I love to listen to good music. I would sit for hours listening to my favorite Christian groups growing up. I even installed an 8-track tape player (remember those?) in my '69 Pontiac LeMans with baby moon chrome hubcaps, so I could take my tunes with me on the road. Over time my love for music has been somewhat replaced by my love for quiet time with the Lord. Don't get me wrong…I still love great music but my desire to be still in the Lord's presence is much greater! There's something about quietness in God's presence that is so overwhelming…so freeing. We get up in arms about so many things. Our lives can become cluttered with noise to the point that we can't even begin to hear the still small voice of God. I've met many who turn the music and noise up so loud to just try and drown out the mess that is going on inside of their lives. They have no peace within. Sometimes when I get to the point that I think God is not going to step in and do something or I think He's not moving fast enough, I can get all frustrated and worried about how things are looking and turning out. I even wonder if He's up there and knows what's going on at all! That's when the words of this Psalm break into my spirit! Be still…quiet yourself my soul and know that He is God! He says, "I am God! I WILL be exalted among the nations, I WILL be exalted in the earth. You don't have to worry yourself. I AM GOD! I can handle things. You just still yourself and know this." How freeing it is to just quietly say to myself, "Shhhhhh…Be still my soul. He is God and He can handle it!"

"Lord I quiet myself today in Your presence. I will still my soul and focus on You. You are God! You will be exalted! Your kingdom will come, Your will shall be done! I will not fret when things seem out of control. I will put my trust in You and You alone! Quiet my spirit today and reassure me. You are God...You are my God! You will be exalted in the earth! I love You Lord! Amen."

"Life-long impact!"

Numbers 6:23-27

²³ "Tell Aaron and his sons, 'This is how you are to bless the Israelites. Say to them:

²⁴ ""The LORD bless you
and keep you;
²⁵ the LORD make his face shine upon you
and be gracious to you;
²⁶ the LORD turn his face toward you and give you
peace."' ²⁷ "So they will put my name on the Israelites,
and I will bless them."

I'm not sure any of us fully understand the power of our words. If I asked you to tell me the names you were called as a youngster I guarantee that you could come up with at least a few of them in a flash! I know I sure can. Some people still live with the pain of 'wounding words' many years later. What was spoken to them or over them has molded and shaped their destinies in a very negative way. How powerful our words are! As a leader, in whatever capacity you find yourself, you have unbelievable power in your tongue! The words you speak to those in your care are a binding and shaping force! What could happen if we would begin to speak words of blessing over those we come in contact with? How amazingly powerful would that be?

I remember one Wednesday night after church our little son Elijah came running up to me with a huge smile on his face. He was ecstatic! He said, "Dad, guess what? My teacher says I'm an ARTIST!" He then proceeded to show me the drawing he had made in his class that night. His teacher had spoken a word of blessing over him and for the next several years of his life he drew everything he saw! That word of blessing spoken in a fleeting moment impacted Elijah for years to come! He's still artistic to this day! Why not speak a word of blessing over someone today! I guarantee it will have impact for years to come!

"Lord help me to put Your blessing and Your name on those I come in contact with and have influence over. May the words of my mouth and the meditation of my heart be pleasing in Your sight Oh Lord today! Please put Your words in my mouth and help me to speak blessings on everyone I meet. I know that You have a plan and purpose for everyone on the face of the earth and I just want my words to be a catalyst for their future. Guard my tongue in Jesus' Name. I will speak for You today. Amen."

"Time to move yet?"

Numbers 9:15-19

[15] On the day the tabernacle, the Tent of the Testimony, was set up, the cloud covered it. From evening till morning the cloud above the tabernacle looked like fire. [16] That is how it continued to be; the cloud covered it, and at night it looked like fire. [17] Whenever the cloud lifted from above the Tent, the Israelites set out; wherever the cloud settled, the Israelites encamped. [18] At the LORD's command the Israelites set out, and at his command they encamped. As long as the cloud stayed over the tabernacle, they remained in camp. [19] When the cloud remained over the tabernacle a long time, the Israelites obeyed the LORD's order and did not set out.

Can you imagine having the God of the universe directing your every move…literally? Talk about a flawless GPS system! All they had to do was to follow the cloud. None of this "Recalculating" business! Just follow the cloud! No agenda for today except to follow the cloud! How simple that sounds and yet we have the same GPS available to us today. God's Holy Spirit will guide and direct us as we listen to His still small voice. No, there's no cloud to follow, but it's the same principle. All I have to do is tune my ear into His frequency and obey what He says. I know a few people who have followed a GPS system that sent them the wrong way…it actually got confused! There's no confusion with the Lord! He knows where you need to be and when you need to be there! He has perfect timing and is always spot on! Sure takes the frustration out of life doesn't it? When we were preparing to plant a church in an area that we had never been to before and hadn't met a soul, we were a bit intimidated. I asked a friend of mine some questions in search of something to calm my fears. He told me something that I've never forgotten. He said, "God has people there that are just waiting for you to show up!" Looking back years later I know it was true! God knows exactly where we need to be at any given moment and He is directing our steps and others as well so that we collide in heavenly perfection! What are you trying to do? Where do you think you need to go? Frustrated? Why not wait on the Lord. Don't move without God! Follow His lead. When you finally arrive, you'll be glad you did!

"Lord I thank You that You care so much about me. You know everything there is about me and You want the best for me. I once again yield my life to You! Guide me Holy Spirit. Tune my ear into Your Holy frequency so that I can hear Your voice clearly. I will not move without You Lord! I want to be always in Your presence. I will follow Your lead. Father You know best! I will move with You! Amen."

"I Am Able!"

Numbers 11:21-23

21 But Moses said, "Here I am among six hundred thousand men on foot, and you say, 'I will give them meat to eat for a whole month!' 22 Would they have enough if flocks and herds were slaughtered for them? Would they have enough if all the fish in the sea were caught for them?"

23 The LORD answered Moses, "Is the LORD's arm too short? You will now see whether or not what I say will come true for you."

The Israelites were craving meat. They had manna for breakfast, manna for lunch and manna for supper…manna, manna, manna! They were tired of manna and were longing for the tastes they once enjoyed in Egypt. Forget the fact that God was feeding them everyday and taking care of their every need…they wanted MEAT! I wonder how many times in my life I have done the same thing…longed for past pleasures. Crazy huh? Anyway, Moses had a chat with God and God had already heard His people grumbling. He hears everything you know! He's even got a bead on the motives in our heart that no one else can see.

So, God says He's going to feed them meat…lots of meat! Not just for a day or two but for a whole month! Well that messed up Moses' brain. How is God going to pull that off? Is He serious? Is it even possible? "We're in the desert for crying out loud!" He even tried to figure it out and came to the conclusion that there was simply no way this could happen. You've been there haven't you? I sure have. I've spent countless hours of wasted time worrying that God couldn't possibly do what He said He would do. I love God's response to Moses; "Is the LORD's arm too short? Seriously…haven't I already shown you time after time that I can handle each and every situation?" What drives us to thinking that God is not able? Is it our lack of faith? You decide for yourself. I think we all know the rest of the story…God came through in a big way. He always does when we put our trust in Him! Why not trust Him today? Is the LORD's arm too short? I think not!

"Lord I know that You are able to do far beyond what I can even ask or think! I will not turn back. The former pleasures in my life are empty. I will trust and obey You and You alone. Give me all that I need today to step forth boldly into all that You have for me. Give me a heart that only longs for You. I know that You are able to handle every situation I encounter. You are an Awesome God and I love You! Amen."

"Right Wise Living."

Proverbs 11:4

**⁴ Wealth is worthless in the day of wrath,
but righteousness delivers from death.**

Wealth seems to give most people a sense of entitlement and empowerment. "I have money, therefore I…" you fill in the blank. If you had a choice to be wealthy or righteous before God, I hope you'd choose the latter. Yes money can buy you a whole lot of stuff in this world. You can purchase things and experiences that will give you some happiness for the time being. The problem is that when the things get old and the experiences wear off you are still left with whatever is happening on the inside of you…the forever stuff! I know people who have everything this world has to offer and yet they are so empty on the inside. They search and search for the latest thing that just might fill that emptiness gnawing within. How crazy is that? You can buy temporary things but you can't buy the things that are eternal…such as peace or eternal salvation! As the wise man said, "Wealth is worthless in the day of wrath, but righteousness delivers from death." Wealth will get you only so far in this life, but righteousness is good for this life and for the life to come! What is righteousness? Righteousness is being in right standing with God. It is being right-wise in your everyday living. We can't live that way on our own…we need the Righteous One, Jesus Christ sitting on the throne of our lives to be truly righteous. He is our righteousness! And yes, He delivers us from death! Hallelujah! What a Savior! If there is something out of whack between you and God then start today by making it right! I know you're probably going to work today to make a living, but why not go before the throne of God today to make a LIFE!

"Lord I don't want to just make a living…I want to make a life! I want to live in such a way that is completely pleasing to You! Help me focus on what is eternal today. Align my life so that it is in harmony with You and Your ways. Take my desire for wealth and make it a desire for You because You are worth so much more than all that this world has to offer. I love You Lord and I place You on the throne of my life today! I will walk right with You. Amen."

"Standing in the Gap!"

Numbers 16:41-48

41 The next day the whole Israelite community grumbled against Moses and Aaron. "You have killed the LORD's people," they said.

42 But when the assembly gathered in opposition to Moses and Aaron and turned toward the Tent of Meeting, suddenly the cloud covered it and the glory of the LORD appeared. 43 Then Moses and Aaron went to the front of the Tent of Meeting, 44 and the LORD said to Moses, 45 "Get away from this assembly so I can put an end to them at once." And they fell facedown.

46 Then Moses said to Aaron, "Take your censer and put incense in it, along with fire from the altar, and hurry to the assembly to make atonement for them. Wrath has come out from the LORD; the plague has started." 47 So Aaron did as Moses said, and ran into the midst of the assembly. The plague had already started among the people, but Aaron offered the incense and made atonement for them. 48 He stood between the living and the dead, and the plague stopped.

I'm a Husband, a Father and a Pastor. Each of those roles is filled with joys and challenges. It's overwhelming at times to realize the responsibility that is mine in each of them. I can't tell you how many times I've done what Aaron did here…stood in the gap for someone under my influence and prayed and interceded until the plague in their life stopped. I believe that God has called each of us to that ministry at some point in our lives. He will show us what is going on in someone's life and burden us to intercede on their behalf. What a privilege to stand between the living and the dead and fight on our knees until something changes! We must push through until we see the victory. I've heard it said that 'PUSH' stands for *Pray Until Something Happens*! That's what we must do! Oh, it's hard work and usually comes with very little thanks in this life but the eternal rewards are amazing! I know that when we get to heaven and are able to see everything clearly that we will be overwhelmed by how powerful our prayers have been. Our reward awaits us on the other side! "He stood between the living and the dead, and the plague stopped." God will give you the same results as you fight on your knees in prayer!

"Lord please anoint me today as I intercede for (   ). I can't stand idly by and watch them perish. Give me what I need to push through in prayer until something happens. I won't give up. I will fight because they are worth it. Thank You Lord for hearing and answering my prayers! You are an amazing God! Amen."

"Face the Impossible!"

Luke 1:37

[37] For nothing is impossible with God."

What a statement! What a heavenly reality check! Do you really believe that or is there a corner of doubt in your heart somewhere? Seems like an easy statement to make until you realize the context. The angel Gabriel is telling Mary that she is going to have a baby, the Son of the Living God, even when she's never been with a man. Seriously? Is that possible? Not humanly possible for sure! But with God all things are possible! If God said it then He can do it…it's just as simple as that. Our part is simply believing what God says. As we stand on the other side of that statement we can see the reality of what eventually happened with Mary.

It's much easier to look back and believe than it is to believe ahead of time or in the midst of a crisis or impossible moment! I've been in impossible situations many times in my life and have watched God come through in a big way! Those moments give me courage to believe God for impossible things when I can't see any possible answer. What are you facing today? Is there a mountain in your way? Is there a situation much too big for you? Nothing is impossible with God! It's not just a nice phrase…its rock solid truth! Truth you can build your life on! So go ahead…face your impossibility with this FACT. Nothing is impossible with God!

"Lord I know deep down in my 'knower' that there is nothing too difficult for You. Establish that fact in my heart today. Let nothing sway me. You are God of the impossible. Lord I am facing (   ) today and I need

Your miracle working power to invade my situation! The only way I can face this impossibility is with You by my side. Do what only You can do Lord! There is none like You in all the earth! I commit my way to You Lord. Amen."

Output > Input = Trouble!

"Let's get it together!"

Luke 3:8

[8] Produce fruit in keeping with repentance. And do not begin to say to yourselves, 'We have Abraham as our father.' For I tell you that out of these stones God can raise up children for Abraham.

John the Baptist is my kind of guy…he always said it like it was! He didn't beat around the bush. He called the religious leaders a bunch of snakes! He wasn't impressed with their pious attitudes and fancy dress…and neither was God! God spoke through John the Baptist and used him to set the stage for Jesus to show up on the scene. "Produce fruit in keeping with repentance" he said. Don't just repent and say you're sorry! Let's see some action here! Show what's happened in your heart by what you do on the outside! Then he began to shoot down the theory that just because they had the right pedigree or family tree that they'd be fine with God. John basically said that God doesn't care what your name is or whose family line you came from…He wants children who really love Him! In fact, when we get so caught up in the fact that we are good church goers and start to look down our noses at everyone else…watch out! God can make children for himself out of stones! Seriously! The reality is that He is looking for those whose hearts are fully His! He's not looking to see what your family tree looks like. God doesn't care what kind of heritage you came from or where you've been. He just wants you…all of you! Come on, let's get it together. When you've given your heart fully to Him you WILL produce fruit in keeping with repentance! You can't stay the way you've always been. Things will change in your life! That's good news. No pious platitudes. No remaining the same. We're going forward and are becoming like Jesus!

"Lord I want to be like You in everything I am and do! I can't stay the way I've always been and I need Your help to conquer those things in me that are not of You. Help the fruit of my life to be sweet. Help those I come in contact with today to see You in me. I am going forward with Your help. I will not remain the same in Jesus' Name! I give You my whole heart today. Amen."

"No Namby Pamby Living!"

Psalm 62:11-12

¹¹ **One thing God has spoken,
two things have I heard:
that you, O God, are strong,**
¹² **and that you, O Lord, are loving.
Surely you will reward each person
according to what he has done.**

Have you ever met a man's man? You know the type…in fact maybe you are one! When God shows Himself to our human eyes we will be overwhelmed by who He is for sure. He is all powerful and awesome…a true Man's Man! Strong yet loving. Powerful and passionate. Mighty and yet filled with amazing mercy. David, earlier in this Psalm declares that his soul finds rest in God alone. God alone is his rock and salvation…his fortress that can never be shaken. What an awesome God He is! Steadfast and secure…a steadfast and solid Rock you can build your life on! What a Man's Man! My Grandpa Hollis was that kind of man. He was a man after God's heart that could take on anything you could throw at him. He was a prayer warrior who believed that if God said it then He would do it! I had the privilege of hanging out some with Grandpa when I was growing up. He worked with his hands and was a strong man physically. He also spent much time on his knees before the Lord and was a very strong man spiritually! He worked hard and he prayed hard. He reminded me of God. Strong and yet loving. I wonder if anyone thinks that about me. Am I a man's man or am I just blending in with the crowd? Do I have the godly qualities that set me apart or am I just another human being living on the earth? I want to be just like God…and I want to receive His reward when I see Him face to face! No namby pamby living for me! I'm gonna be a man's man…strong and loving!

"Lord I'm so glad You have put Your hand of blessing on my life! I'm so grateful that You have saved me and changed my life! I do want to be like You Lord! I want to be strong and loving. Fill me up with all that You are Lord. Help me to make a difference in someone's life today. Help me to be an example of who You are in this world...my little world. Thank You Lord. Amen."

"Do what you say!"

Numbers 32:23

[23] "But if you fail to do this, you will be sinning against the LORD; and you may be sure that your sin will find you out.

I don't know if your parents used that line on you or not but mine sure did! "Be sure your sin will find you out!" It sure worked in my life. It originated as a warning from Moses to the Gadites and Reubenites to fulfill what they said they would do. They made a promise to come alongside their brothers and fight for them before they retired to the homes and land that they had chosen for themselves. I've come to realize that it's no big deal to most people to go back on their word anymore. Some people's word is so untrustworthy that you can't put stock in anything they say! Every word that comes out of their mouths is carefully weighed for an ounce of truth and many times comes up lacking. If their words were a water bucket, it would be filled with thousands of holes! Whatever happened to 'My word is my guarantee'? When all is said and done, many times the only thing you have left is your word. Listen, God takes our words seriously! When we don't keep our word we are sinning against the Lord; and you may be sure that your sin will find you out. You can't run from it. Sooner or later your sin will catch up to you. Before you know it the words you have promised and not fulfilled will hunt you down and make you pay full price with interest! Come on…do what you say you're going to do! That's Christ-Like to the core!

"Lord I don't want to be just a 'sayer'…I want to be a 'doer'! Help me to carefully weigh my words today before

I speak. I don't want to sin against You Lord. Help me to understand the importance of what I say and the weight that my words carry. I will speak Your words today and I will follow You with all my heart. I want to be like You Lord! Amen."

Oak trees don't grow overnight, but weeds do!

"Look for the good in everyone!"

Proverbs 11:27

²⁷ He who seeks good finds goodwill, but evil comes to him who searches for it.

You've heard it said, "Behind every cloud there is a silver lining". I'd like to think that inside every "yucky" person or ugly circumstance is something good that just needs to be discovered. It really is true that you find whatever it is that you're looking for. If you are seeking good…you'll find good. If you're looking for evil…you'll definitely find that too! You can pretty much find anything you're searching for if you look hard enough. Your mindset is crucial. I know that I've met some really 'irregular people' in my life and you surely have as well. As soon as I said 'irregular', you probably put a face to it didn't you?

Well we all have those kinds of people in our lives and yet if we dig deep enough we can find something of value in each one of them if we look hard enough. Everyone you meet has something beautiful in them that just might be covered up with all kinds of stuff…ugly stuff…stuff that works hard to hide the beauty that is deep within them. What could happen if we began to seek the good in every one we met? How would our lives change if we began to look for good in every difficult circumstance and situation? You really do find what you're looking for so why not look for good today? Why not turn the 'good searchlight' on and discover the silver lining behind that cloud? Something tells me that your day will be much brighter when you do!

"Lord help me to seek good and not evil. Help me to discover the beauty behind (   ). I really need new lenses to look through…Godly lenses. I confess that my default is to search for the wrong things in (   ). Help me Lord to see what only You can see! Help me to turn the good searchlight on that brings good things to light. This is going to be a great day! Amen."

"Underwear Issues!"

Deuteronomy 6:25

25 And if we are careful to obey all this law before the LORD our God, as he has commanded us, that will be our righteousness."

Did your parents ever tell you to wear clean underwear when you went out? Was their reasoning that you should have clean underwear on in case you were in an accident? I know, right? How crazy is that advice. It's like if you have on dirty underwear and no one knows about it then its ok! Just don't let anyone know that your underwear is dirty and you'll be fine! I'm not sure what that has to do with obedience and righteousness but the mindset of some people is pretty skewed sometimes. If no one knows I'm not being obedient (besides God) then it doesn't really matter! REALLY!?!?! How ridiculous is that?

The longer I live the more I'm convinced that obedience truly is the key to life! It seeps into every crevice of our life just like disobedience will do if we live there. As Moses shares God's commands with the people he says that if they will obey all the law that God has laid down for them then THAT will be their righteousness. Righteousness – being in right standing/relationship with God. When we obey God it brings us in right standing with Him. Do you like it when your kids disobey you? Isn't that frustrating? It sure messes up the relationship doesn't it? God is looking for hearts that are fully His. Don't obey just when someone might be looking (clean underwear)…let your obedience, even when no one is looking, be from the heart! That's right-wise living! By the way…did you change your underwear yet?

"Lord I want to follow Your ways with all I am. Your love for me draws me to You. I want to be in step with You all day long. Please help me know when I'm out of synch with You Lord. Help me to walk carefully before You today...every step of the way. May my heart be fully Yours oh Lord! I really do love You. Amen."

"Contagiously Irresistible Fruit!"

Proverbs 11:30

[30] The fruit of the righteous is a tree of life, and he who wins souls is wise.

Ever bitten into something and gotten the surprise of your life? You expected one thing and were flabbergasted to get something totally the opposite! Fruit can be like that. I've taken a bite of an apple that I was sure would be sweet and my taste buds were violated with sour! I've had the same kind of experience with a few people in my life…supposed Christians I might add. I've come close enough to taste some of the fruit of their lives and have been shocked with what I discovered. How utterly disappointing. When I should have gotten sweet I was assaulted with sour!

The fruit of the righteous is a tree of LIFE. Our lives should produce life in all of its splendor. Life should flow in our words and actions. There should be life in our attitudes and responses. When anyone comes close enough to experience the fruit of our lives they should be pleasantly surprised! The wise man goes on to say that he who wins souls is wise. When our lives are filled with the life of God then the natural by-product is that souls are won to the kingdom of God! You see, that kind of life is irresistible! I've met some people like that and I'm sure you have too. What they have is irresistibly contagious…you can't help but want what they've got! I know others, sad to say, who are the exact opposite. The closer you get to them the more you want to back away and NOT catch what they've got! I've heard people say, "If that's what a Christian is, I don't want anything to do with Christianity!" How sad is that? What kind of fruit are you producing? May the Lord help each of us to bear the right kind of fruit…contagiously irresistible fruit for His kingdom!

"Lord I want to be like You in all my ways. I really desire to have Your contagiously irresistible fruit in my life. Please help me to be the kind of Christian that honors You and reflects You well. Let Your life flow through me to someone today…someone who desperately needs an authentic touch from Your throne of grace. Thank You Lord for making me wise. I love You. Amen."

"God is Smiling!"

[8] At that time the LORD set apart the tribe of Levi to carry the ark of the covenant of the LORD, to stand before the LORD to minister and to pronounce blessings in his name, as they still do today.

You may not be a minister…a paid clergy person, but please indulge me for a moment. God set apart some of His people to do that full-time. It's a high calling. Even if you're not a full-time minister, this scripture gives us a glimpse into what the Lord's ministers are supposed to do and be. The tribe of Levi was set apart to carry the ark of the covenant of the Lord. They were to carry on their shoulders the presence of the Lord. What a responsibility that is. Minister friend, are you carrying with you everywhere you go the presence of Almighty God? Is there a sense that God is with you? Our churches and people need us to carry His presence! We can't do what He's called us to do without His awesome presence in our lives!

He also reminds us that our calling is to stand before the Lord to minister…to serve…and to pronounce blessings in His name. Everything we do is done before the Lord…whether it's done in secret or in public. We will be rewarded by the Lord for what we've done. Everyone doesn't have to see everything you do…God sees and will reward…and His rewards are way better than any reward from any man! I guess the thing that strikes me the biggest is the last line…to pronounce blessings in His name. What a calling…what a high privilege! As I take stock of my preaching and my interaction with people, I have to ask myself if I've pronounced blessings in His name or have I put a huge burden on God's people in His name. Oh, I know there's got to be balance here but if I haven't been pronouncing blessings in a while then something needs to change! God wants to bless His people and we are His spokesperson. If you are a parent or are in leadership of any kind, then maybe just maybe God wants to use you in this way too. He wants you to carry His presence with you as you serve and speak blessings over those in your charge. May His presence go with us as He fills our mouths with His words of blessing. I have a sneaking suspicion that He will smile as we do and so will His people!

"Lord I want to make You smile today! Fill my life with Your awesome presence as I go through this day. May my mouth be filled with the blessings that You want to pronounce over those I come in contact with. I stand before You to minister today. Please give me all that I need Lord. I love You with all my heart and I want to be and do what You want me to be and do. Speak to me so that I can speak to others. Amen."

"Speak up!"

Deuteronomy 11:2

² Remember today that your children were not the ones who saw and experienced the discipline of the LORD your God: his majesty, his mighty hand, his outstretched arm;

It's not their fault…they just haven't seen and experienced what you have! They can't…they haven't lived long enough. That's why you've got to share with them everything you've experienced. Your kids deserve that! They need to know how the Lord has disciplined you so they don't have to go through the same stuff you've gone through. Wisdom is learning from someone else's mistakes so we don't have to be knocked down like they were. You can help your kids and those younger than you by sharing your pain from disobedience! You have the ability to build a bridge that they can walk on over the same situations that you almost drowned in! Show them your scars and let them know how healing came. Tell the story of how God came through for you. What a high responsibility and privilege that is. They haven't experienced His majesty like you have…His mighty hand, His outstretched arm! These young ones don't know the power of God quite yet. They will someday experience His amazing might, but in the meantime tell them the stories. Speak of what you've seen and heard. Tell them your story. Don't hold back. They need your experience to spark a spirit of faith in them for the same thing! Has God done a miracle in your life or in the life of someone you know? Speak it out! Tell them! For all they know, God is just a figment of your imagination…a bedtime story that doesn't really affect their lives at all. Tell them the truth! Tell them the miracles you've seen and experienced first hand. Speak up! Someday they'll have a story of their own to tell!

"Lord please open my eyes to see all that You've done for me. Help me to speak out boldly and share my story and the stories about You that I know are true. What great miracles I've experienced in my life. I will boldly declare Your wondrous works to the next generation Lord. Give my children and grandchildren stories to tell of Your greatness in their lives. You are Majestic Oh Lord and Mighty! I praise You today for all You are and for all You have done! Amen."

"Stay out of God's chair!"

Deuteronomy 32:39

**[39] "See now that I myself am He!
There is no god besides me.
I put to death and I bring to life,
I have wounded and I will heal,
and no one can deliver out of my hand.**

Repeat after me..."You, Oh Lord are God and I am not!"
Repeat it again out loud..."You, Oh Lord are God and I am
not!" There now, doesn't that release a lot of stress from your
life? Sometimes we get to acting like we're God and that really
messes things up. If I was God I would...fill in the blank. Oh I
know we don't really say it, but in our minds we so many times
have contemplated the perfect scenario and then began to
pray fervently for God to do what we think He ought to do.
And then when He doesn't answer our prayers we get ticked!
Why? Because we had it all figured out didn't we. We didn't
say that we were God, but we sure acted like it. I've heard it
said that "If you want to get along with God then you need to
stay out of His chair!" I don't think we consciously take over
the throne but we sure seem to drift that way. I meet people
all the time who are spittin' mad at God. They are so angry
with God that they say they could never trust Him again! They
are so hurt and wounded by the God who was supposed to
love them. When you dig down to the reason why they're so
mad, it almost always stems from an 'unanswered prayer'.
God didn't answer their prayer the way that they thought He
should! They knew better than Him what should have
happened! Let me see now...if I'm God and He's not then I
can just tell Him what to do right? On the other hand if He's
God and I'm not then I must submit my will to His will and stay
off of His throne! The reality is that it's a much better way to
live letting God be God. "See now that I myself am He! There
is no god besides Me." Says the Lord!

"Lord I do realize that You are God and there is none besides You. I really don't want to be God but my actions sure drift that way some days. Please help me to place You on the throne of my life each and every day. You know what I can never know and I submit my life to You. You are God and I am not! Rule and reign in me Lord! I bow at Your feet and worship You and You alone! Amen."

"LIFE!"

Deuteronomy 32:47

47 They are not just idle words for you—they are your life. By them you will live long in the land you are crossing the Jordan to possess."

"I brought you into this world and I can take you out of it!" Some parents have used that line on their kids when they don't obey their rules. When our children obey what we've said, life is sweet in the house. When they choose to go against our words then watch out, there is war in the camp! Moses was laying out the law of God to His people and he finishes with this statement, "They are not just idle words for you – they are your life." God's not just laying all of this down because He wants to just have an idle chat with you. He's not giving you these instructions so He can make your life miserable and you won't be able to have any fun. No, He cares deeply for you and He knows what is best for you. Just like a parent is able to see things a young child is incapable of seeing, our God is all-knowing, all-seeing, all-wise and cares deeply that we live to our fullest capacity! He's laying out some boundaries and guidelines for you to follow so that you will live long in the land that He is giving to you as an inheritance. He wants you to have an abundant life…life to the fullest extent possible! These words of God, these rules for living ARE your life! If we would just listen and obey then our lives would be so much better. To follow the word of the Lord is to better yourself and your life capacity. The enemy of your soul wants to steal, kill and destroy you. He is out to rob you of everything Father God has for you. If he can get you to shrug off the words of God then he has accomplished his mission. Jesus said that He has come to give us LIFE…life to the fullest…abundant life! Real life filled with the blessing and favor of the Lord! Come on, obey His words…they are your LIFE!

"Lord I really want to follow You and Your ways. Help me not to listen to the taunts of the devil and give in to the pull of this world. Fill me with Your words of life. I know that You have amazing plans for me. I will listen to Your words and obey what You say! I know You see what I cannot see and so I will follow Your voice. You will lead me to my desired haven. I love You Lord. Amen."

"Bring relief to a weary soul!"

Proverbs 12:25

**25 An anxious heart weighs a man down,
but a kind word cheers him up.**

You've met them before I'm sure…a person with an anxious heart. Their whole demeanor yells it out. Their shoulders stoop down; it seems the weight of the world is on them. You may have been there at one point in your life too…when the cares of this world become too much to bear and you find yourself with an anxious, heavy heart. An anxious heart is difficult to carry around. It really does weigh you down. It feels like you have added 100 lbs. to your life. Have you ever been there? I know I have. There have been moments in my usually amazing life that I feel the weight of certain things pressing in. I don't know how to explain it but it seems that the more you try to push it off the heavier it becomes. What's the cure for the anxious heart? A kind word! Once again that little muscle inside your mouth has amazing power in it. A kind word spoken at just the right time is filled with releasing power. You have the ability to set someone free from the weight of their situation if even for a moment. This past Valentines Day we as a church went and "kissed" our community. It's amazing what a simple, kind gesture can do to make someone's day. An inexpensive flower, a few pieces of chocolate, a kind word, a smile with a word of encouragement…priceless! It was amazing how that simple little act of kindness meant so much to those who were heavy hearted. Tears even flowed from some. What simple thing can you do today to lift someone else? Is there a kind word that needs to be expressed to someone you're going to brush shoulders with? Possibly a small, simple act of kindness that will lift someone's heaviness? Open your eyes to the possibilities. Maybe, just maybe, the Lord wants you to be on the lookout today and arm you with a kind word that will bring relief to a weary soul!

"Lord open my eyes today to someone in need of a kind word. Let me be Your mouthpiece to speak life. I know what it is to have an anxious heart and I want to bring relief to those You bring my way. Thank You Lord for the times You've lifted my heavy heart. Fill my mouth with the words You want me to speak to those in need. Empty my mouth of worthless talk. I will speak words of life today in Jesus' Name! Amen."

"Close Proximity!"

Deuteronomy 34:9

⁹ Now Joshua son of Nun was filled with the spirit of wisdom because Moses had laid his hands on him. So the Israelites listened to him and did what the LORD had commanded Moses.

There is something about close proximity that brings an impartation. There are some things you learn simply by osmosis. Osmosis is defined as, "the gradual, often unconscious, absorption of knowledge or ideas through continual exposure rather than deliberate learning." My Dad is a minister and I grew up absorbing his way of doing things simply by being around him so much. There are some things I just know to do in ministry because I was around my Dad when he did them. Thanks Dad!

You can learn good things by osmosis but you can also pick up some bad things through continual exposure. There is also the mysterious miracle of imparting something to someone through the laying on of hands. That's a God thing! This seems to be the case here with Moses and Joshua. Although Joshua had learned a lot from Moses by osmosis, there was a deliberate laying on of his hands here to impart a spirit of wisdom to him.

Who have you been gleaning from lately? Leaders are readers you know. Are you a reader? Leaders are also good followers. Do you have someone in your life who is ahead of you in the faith…someone who you can imitate their faith? I think that's a vital missing link in many leaders' lives. They are out ahead, on their own, without anyone beyond them pouring into their life. You need a Moses in your life…someone who can teach you a thing or two. You need someone who has been where you are going and who will lay their hands on you purposefully and impart whatever the Spirit of the Lord would have them impart to you. You also need a Joshua, someone behind you that you are imparting what you've been blessed with. Lay hands on them with purpose and watch what God will do! Close proximity is powerful!

"Lord please use me to pour into someone today. Show me what to say, what to do and what I should be to them. Use me in whatever way You choose. Give me the wisdom and discernment I need in each and every situation. I want to be a leader that follows well...I want to be a good follower of You Lord. Teach me Your ways and I will walk in Your paths. Amen."

"Open wide your mouth!"

Psalm 81:10

**[10] I am the LORD your God,
who brought you up out of Egypt.
Open wide your mouth and I will fill it.**

If God can set you free from your sin then He can take care of all your other needs as well! I'm not sure where we got to thinking that God could forgive our sins but couldn't do anything else for us. He says, "I am the LORD your God, who brought you up out of Egypt…I set you free from the bondage you were in! I sent a deliverer and rescued you! Food? No problem! Open wide your mouth and I will fill it! Shelter? Never an issue…I can take care of your every need if you'll just trust me!" He's an awesome God and He is able to provide everything we need. We have a new puppy in our house. His name is Sullivan Theodore Hollis and he's a gorgeous cream colored Chow Chow. He relies on us to feed him every day and guess what? We've never let him down! All he does is open wide his mouth and we fill it! We're also going to be Grandparents very soon. I've been around enough babies to know that when they're hungry all they have to do is open wide their mouth and their loving parents will fill it. Don't you think that your Heavenly Father will do the same for you? There's another part to this passage that ignites me. There are times in my life that I don't know what to say…situations that call for a word of wisdom from above. I take God at His word, breathe a prayer and open wide my mouth. Miraculously He fills it every time! What an awesome God we serve! He cares about every detail of our lives and intervenes when we need Him most! Go ahead…open wide your mouth…He will fill it!

"Lord I do need You today. You've never let me down and I know You won't begin to today. I put my whole trust and faith in You. You know every need in my life and my life is in Your hands. Thank You for intervening in my behalf. Thank You for providing everything I need as I trust in You. You have forgiven me of my sin and then done so much more for me. I am overwhelmed by You Lord. I love you with all my heart! Amen."

"Who you hangin' out with?"

Proverbs 13:20

**[20] He who walks with the wise grows wise,
but a companion of fools suffers harm.**

You know what they say, "Birds of a feather flock together!"
Well I guess I would say to you what kind of bird do you
WANT to be? The choice really is yours. You can become
anything you want to become if you'll begin to hang out with
the right people! I've seen it my whole life…people come in to
a church and you have high, high hopes for them. Before you
know it they start hanging out with the wrong crowd. That's
right…there's a wrong crowd even in the church! They get
embroiled in all the mess that comes with whatever crowd
they choose to associate with and find themselves entangled
in all kinds of sticky webs. He who walks with the wise grows
wise!

You can choose to hang out with wise folks anywhere you go.
I know that we are all drawn to different kinds of people but if
we would set our internal compass to wisdom then any foolish
thing or person would repel and repulse us. I think that is one
of the greatest gifts my parents gave me growing up. They
showed me how to recognize a fool…even in church! They
would point out the behavior of certain people and explain the
foolishness or wisdom of each…the end results of their
choices. They showed me the path of people's decisions and
where that pathway led…good and bad.

Andy Stanley says, "This is a path and it leads somewhere!"
Drinking alcohol is a path and it leads somewhere. Drugs,
cigarettes, riotous living, the party scene, etc. are all paths
that lead somewhere you don't want to end up! There is a
path of wisdom as well and it leads to a blessed life! I am so
grateful that my parents took the time to show me that he who

walks with the wise grows wise, but a companion of fools suffers harm. They saved me from many messes in my lifetime! They set me on the right path. What about you? Who you hangin' out with? What path are you on? Maybe it's time for a wake-up call and a change of companions and direction!

"Lord I don't want to end up where the fool ends up. I've had enough harm in my life. I choose today, with Your help, to set my inner compass to wisdom! Help me to see clearly. Please give me the wisdom that I need to make wise choices. I will walk with You Lord for You are true wisdom. Guide me down the pathway that leads to life...everlasting life! Thank You Lord! I love You with all my heart. Amen."

"Love or Hate?"

Proverbs 13:24

**[24] He who spares the rod hates his son,
but he who loves him is careful to discipline him.**

My Dad used to say to us before he spanked us, "This is going to hurt me more than it hurts you." I would always think to myself, "Yeah, Right! Are you kidding me?" That was before I became a father and understood the intense pain of lovingly disciplining and correcting my own children. Here is one of those parenting proverbs that really hits hard. The wise man says that if you don't discipline your child, you are actually telling him that you hate him! I've heard it said that the Lord loves you just the way you are…He just loves you way too much to let you stay like that! It's the same thing in parenting. How cruel it is for us as parents to allow destructive behavior patterns to become ingrained in our children. Behavior patterns that will be very difficult to correct the older they get. It is much more loving to use careful, quick and loving discipline with them so that they aren't shackled down by things that will eventually destroy their lives if left unchecked.

Discipline of any kind is never fun. Whether it's your children or your employee or someone you care deeply for…discipline is always difficult. But discipline filled with love and focused intently on helping them become what they need to be can be the most loving thing you can do as a leader or a parent. If you really love them, you'll discipline them. I always told my children, "I'm doing this because I love you. I love you too much to let you act like that…because you're better than that!" There are some things I do as a pastor because I love my people too much to let them act that way. Love or hate? You decide.

"Lord I need You to guide me as I discipline my children and those You've placed under my care. Give me wisdom to see what needs to change and how to change it. Please help me not to be too harsh. Let my loving discipline be carefully administered with Your grace. I want to be like You Lord in all I say and do! Help me to be the leader/parent you want me to be. In Jesus' Name. Amen."

Deuteronomy 32:2

**Let my teaching fall like rain
and my words descend like dew,
like showers on new grass,
like abundant rain on tender plants.**